KETO KITCHEN
AIR FRYER
COOKBOOK

MORE THAN 100 HEALTHY FRIED RECIPES
FOR THE KETOGENIC DIET

ELLA SANDERS

CASTLE POINT BOOKS
NEW YORK

KETO KITCHEN: AIR FRYER COOKBOOK.
Copyright © 2020 by St. Martin's Press.
All rights reserved. Printed in the United States of America.
For information, address St. Martin's Press, 120 Broadway, New York, NY 10271.

www.castlepointbooks.com

The Castle Point Books trademark is owned by Castle Point Publications, LLC.
Castle Point books are published and distributed by St. Martin's Press.

ISBN 978-1-250-25341-5 (trade paperback)
ISBN 978-1-250-25340-8 (ebook)

Design by Tara Long

Images used under license from Shutterstock.com

Our books may be purchased in bulk for promotional, educational, or business use.
Please contact your local bookseller or the Macmillan Corporate and
Premium Sales Department at 1-800-221-7945, extension 5442, or by email at
MacmillanSpecialMarkets@macmillan.com.

First Edition: January 2020

10 9 8 7 6 5 4 3 2 1

CONTENTS

INTRODUCTION

YOU CAN LOSE WEIGHT WHILE INDULGING in luscious Fried Cheesecake Bites (page 146). Boost your metabolism while dining on home-style Southern Fried Drumsticks (page 24) and Marinated Steak Tips with Mushrooms (page 55). Burn fat while munching on crispy mozzarella sticks (page 127) and chicken wings (page 122). The secret: a ketogenic diet that focuses on keeping you satisfied and energized with just the right amount of healthy fats paired with your air fryer that puts you in complete control of how much fat is added to your food during cooking. Welcome to the dynamic duo for losing weight while enjoying food that tastes amazing!

WEIGHT LOSS MAGIC WITH A KETOGENIC DIET

Given up on diets because they're so difficult to follow? Too much sacrifice with little results and constant hunger? You'll love the ketogenic plan! For years it was studied as a way to help people with epilepsy control their seizures. But along the way, experts also noticed a ketogenic diet promoted reliable weight loss as well.

How does it work? With a focus on the right balance of fats versus carbs, eating the keto way guides your body into *ketosis*, a metabolic state in which your body uses ketones (taken from the fat you eat, as well as body fat) as its primary fuel source instead of glucose (from carbohydrates). When your body enters this fat-burning state, you naturally lower your blood sugar levels, which may be beneficial if you are at risk for developing diabetes. Low-carb diets have also been shown to help lower bad cholesterol levels and reduce high blood pressure, factors that may play a role in reducing the risk of heart disease.

In this collection of recipes, you may find it helpful to take note of the following:

EGGS AND DAIRY. Unless otherwise specified, use large eggs. And because a ketogenic weight loss plan relies on the right ratio of fats in your diet, avoid reduced-fat dairy products unless the recipe specifies otherwise. As for butter, use unsalted butter in your cooking; it is better to add a small amount of salt to a dish as you cook rather than rely on salty ingredients to enhance the flavor of your cooking.

MEATS AND POULTRY. Some proponents of ketogenic weight loss encourage using organic, grass-fed, or free-range animal products whenever possible; the choice is yours to make.

OLIVE OIL. Use extra-virgin olive oil when you desire a more pronounced flavor in the finished dish (such as in a salad); however, unless otherwise specified, the choice is up to you and your budget.

SWERVE. There are many granulated sugar replacements that claim they are zero-carbohydrate foods because the small amount they do contain is indigestible. These recipes call for a readily available brand of sugar replacement called Swerve that looks and tastes very much like the real thing, but you can use any similar sugar-free product.

Additional benefits of a ketogenic weight loss plan:

A FOCUS ON WHOLE FOODS. To help the body reach a state of ketosis, you'll want to focus on eating whole foods as much as possible, especially those low in carbohydrates and rich in healthy fats. That means you can enjoy olive oil, eggs, avocados, nuts, full-fat cheeses, and even the occasional butter splurge in your cooking! When it comes to vegetables, you can enjoy practically anything provided it isn't too starchy. Greens, mushrooms, broccoli, cabbage, cucumbers, tomatoes, zucchini, and yellow squash are all low-carb superstars.

AMAZING SATISFACTION. Because the ketogenic diet emphasizes healthy fats, it helps you feel full faster. And without the sudden insulin spikes that go along with eating lots of carbohydrates, you are far less likely to feel the usual hunger pangs we typically associate with trying to lose weight.

LOTS OF CHOICES. In general, to achieve ketosis you should simply aim to get no more than 50 grams of carbohydrates a day and make sure that 70 percent of your calories are coming from fat. That leaves plenty of room to make selections that you enjoy and that fit with all of your health goals. Remember that it's always smart to talk with your doctor before starting any weight loss plan, especially if you are living with a chronic health condition such as diabetes or heart disease. If you have seizures and are curious to try a ketogenic diet to see if they might be lessened, talk with your doctor to determine the carbohydrate goal that is best for you.

The recipes in this collection provide nutrition facts to help you keep track of macronutrients and calculate your overall daily intake. They also indicate the percentage of calories drawn from each macronutrient. You'll see that not every dish contains 70 percent of its calories from fat, but many contain more than that amount. Over the course of your day, strive for balance by eating a variety of low-carb foods.

Some air fryers come with special equipment such as baking pans for pizzas and desserts. However, you can use any glass, metal, or silicone baking dishes with your air fryer as long as they fit in the basket and don't block the circulation of hot air. Here are some other key items you'll want to have on hand:

OLIVE OIL SPRAY. Instead of using nonstick cooking spray, which may over time compromise the integrity of nonstick surfaces, consider purchasing a pump-style spray bottle that you can fill with regular olive oil. Some foods will benefit from a light coating of oil before baking.

PARCHMENT PAPER. Treated with a thin layer of silicone, parchment paper provides a nonstick surface for foods that might otherwise slip through the holes of your air fryer basket. When lining your basket with parchment, avoid cutting a piece so large that it covers all the holes (otherwise air will not circulate properly).

MEAT THERMOMETER. While the recipes in this collection offer visual hints to know what your food should look like when it's done, the only way to know for sure whether meats are cooked to a safe temperature is to rely on a meat thermometer.

TONGS. Although it's possible to simply give many foods a quick shake in the basket to ensure even cooking, some foods will require deliberate turning. Tongs are helpful for this task.

To minimize carbohydrates in the foods you eat, steer away from the following:

- all grains and beans (including wheat flour, bread, pasta, and rice)

- all sweet and starchy vegetables (avoid all potatoes, peas, corn, and beets; limit onions and sweet peppers)

- all fruits (except berries)

- alcohol (including wine)

- added sugar (including honey, syrup, and agave nectar; read labels carefully to avoid anything with sugar or high fructose corn syrup)

That may sound like a tall order, but take a look at the recipes in this collection. You'll see that eating the keto way doesn't require sacrificing flavor or even the traditionally high-carb foods you love, such as pizza, muffins, chicken parm, cupcakes, and brownies. With smart ingredient swaps and the help of your air fryer, you'll love what you eat while you lose weight!

KETO MADE EASY WITH YOUR AIR FRYER

Now that you're amazed by how powerful a keto eating style can be for weight loss and improved health, get ready to see how your air fryer comes into the picture. Air fryers are revolutionary countertop appliances that make it even easier and more delicious to follow a ketogenic diet for weight loss. What's the secret? Air fryers circulate hot air to cook foods, which gives them the same crisp exterior and tender interior produced by conventional deep fryers without the need to submerge your food in cooking oils. Beyond frying, the air fryer can also roast, steam, grill, and bake. Whatever cooking method you turn to the air fryer for, it improves the process with faster, more even heat—and delicious results. The benefits you get with an air fryer:

CRISP FLAVOR. Even with the low-carb ingredients the ketogenic diet emphasizes, you can achieve terrific texture. The air fryer is a game changer for your favorite foods, like the Chicken

Croquettes with Creole Sauce on page 38 or the Crab Cakes with Lemon Aioli on page 74. Are desserts your passion? Then don't miss the Air-Fried Doughnut Bites on page 151 or the Guilt-Free Chocolate Chip Cookies on page 138.

SPEEDY COOKING. Not only do air fryers tend to speed the cooking time for most recipes (the circulation of hot air means foods cook faster), but you'll also find that using an air fryer usually involves less hassle than traditional cooking methods. Need to check for doneness? Just slide open the basket to take a quick look. Need to turn the food to ensure even baking? Give the basket a quick shake. That said, models vary, so use the cooking times in this collection as a guide versus a rule and adjust accordingly.

LESS MESS. Air frying is considerably less messy than deep-fat frying. The units are self-contained, so you don't need to contend with splatters. And because most air-fryer baskets come with a nonstick coating, cleanup is a breeze.

COMFORT AND CONVENIENCE. Baking with a conventional oven during the summer months is a sure-fire way to heat up your whole kitchen in a hurry. But given their compact size, air fryers simply don't give off that much heat. Many models also come with preset features for baking certain types of foods at the press of a button. Essentially, there are few things that you can make in a conventional oven that you can't make even more easily in an air fryer. The only challenge is that because the units are smaller, sometimes you may need to cook a recipe in batches.

With your air fryer and a ketogenic diet, you can make your favorite fried foods healthy and make weight loss easy. Ready to get started? In the chapters that follow, you'll find more than 100 delicious recipes (including snacks and desserts!) that show you how to master an air fryer while following a ketogenic eating plan. Start your morning with Breakfast Pizza (page 15) that will fill you up and have you bursting with energy. Snack on Cheese Crisps (page 124) to keep you and your metabolism going strong until your next meal. Watch your air fryer make crispy Classic Fish Sticks (page 80) that you can feel good about eating. You'll be amazed by how fast and simple it is to make flavorful foods that actually boost your weight-loss and fat-burning success!

BREAKFASTS

KETO GRANOLA

You don't need to give up the ease and crunch of a cereal breakfast while following a ketogenic meal plan. Your air fryer is a great tool for whipping up a crispy batch of low-carb granola to fulfill that craving. Just go easy on the milk; ½ cup of whole milk has 6 grams of carbs.

½ cup pecans, coarsely chopped

½ cup walnuts or almonds, coarsely chopped

¼ cup unsweetened flaked coconut

¼ cup almond flour

¼ cup ground flaxseed or chia seeds

2 tablespoons sunflower seeds

2 tablespoons melted butter

¼ cup Swerve sugar replacement

½ teaspoon ground cinnamon

½ teaspoon vanilla extract

¼ teaspoon ground nutmeg

¼ teaspoon salt

2 tablespoons water

1. Preheat the air fryer to 250°F. Cut a piece of parchment paper to fit inside the air fryer basket.

2. In a large bowl, toss the nuts, coconut, almond flour, ground flaxseed or chia seeds, sunflower seeds, butter, Swerve, cinnamon, vanilla, nutmeg, salt, and water until thoroughly combined.

3. Spread the granola on the parchment paper and flatten to an even thickness.

4. Air fry for about an hour, or until golden throughout. Remove from the air fryer and allow to fully cool. Break the granola into bite-size pieces and store in a covered container for up to a week.

PER SERVING
305 CALORIES
8 G PROTEIN (10%)
10 G CARBS (12%)
28 G FAT (78%)   6 G SAT FAT
6 G FIBER

BLT BREAKFAST WRAP

Bacon is keto-friendly and extremely easy to cook until it's perfectly crisp in the air fryer. If you don't need four servings at once, cook the bacon ahead of time, refrigerate what you'd like to save, and reheat a few pieces at a time as you need them in just a few minutes.

8 ounces (about 12 slices) reduced-sodium bacon

8 tablespoons mayonnaise

8 large romaine lettuce leaves

4 Roma tomatoes, sliced

Salt and freshly ground black pepper

1. Arrange the bacon in a single layer in the air fryer basket. (It's OK if the bacon sits a bit on the sides.) Set the air fryer to 350°F and cook for 10 minutes. Check for crispiness and cook for 2 to 3 minutes longer if needed. Cook in batches, if necessary, and drain the grease in between batches.

2. Spread 1 tablespoon of mayonnaise on each of the lettuce leaves and top with the tomatoes and cooked bacon. Season to taste with salt and freshly ground black pepper. Roll the lettuce leaves as you would a burrito, securing with a toothpick if desired.

PER SERVING
370 CALORIES
11 G PROTEIN (12%)
7 G CARBS (7%)
34 G FAT (81%)   7 G SAT FAT
3 G FIBER

EGGS IN HAM CUPS

Looking for a simple yet satisfying brunch that keeps you in the keto zone? This dish is sure to get rave reviews for easy prep and great taste. Use silicone baking cups, which will fit better in an air fryer basket than a traditional muffin tin.

1. Preheat the air fryer to 400°F. Lightly coat 4 silicone muffin cups with vegetable oil.

2. Line each cup with a piece of ham, tearing it into a few smaller pieces, if necessary, to ensure an even fit. (It's OK if the ham extends slightly above the top of the cup.) Sprinkle 1 tablespoon of cheese into the bottom of each cup, then crack an egg into each.

3. Air fry for 12 to 15 minutes until the whites are set and the yolk is cooked to the desired doneness. Scatter parsley on top, if desired, and season to taste with salt and pepper.

4 slices deli ham

¼ cup shredded Cheddar cheese

4 large eggs

1 tablespoon chopped fresh parsley (optional)

Salt and freshly ground black pepper

PER SERVING
280 CALORIES
26 G PROTEIN (38%)
2 G CARBS (3%)
18 G FAT (59%)   7 G SAT FAT
0 G FIBER

SCOTCH EGGS
WITH SMOKY MUSTARD SAUCE

MAKES 8 SERVINGS

Scotch eggs traditionally receive a bread crumb coating and deep frying. With this air-fried version, you avoid the extra carbs and calories. Make sure you read the labels on your sausage carefully; breakfast sausages often contain syrup and other added sugars.

1. Preheat the air fryer to 390°F.

2. Divide the sausage into 8 portions. Take each portion of sausage, pat it down into a patty, and place 1 egg in the middle, gently wrapping the sausage around the egg until the egg is completely covered. (Wet your hands slightly if you find the sausage to be too sticky.) Repeat with the remaining eggs and sausage.

3. In a small shallow bowl, whisk the egg and milk until frothy. In another shallow bowl, place the crushed pork rinds. Working one at a time, dip a sausage-wrapped egg into the beaten egg and then into the pork rinds, gently rolling to coat evenly. Repeat with the remaining sausage-wrapped eggs.

4. Arrange the eggs in a single layer in the air fryer basket, and lightly spray with olive oil. Air fry for 10 to 12 minutes, pausing halfway through the baking time to turn the eggs, until the eggs are hot and the sausage is cooked through.

5. To make the sauce: In a small bowl, combine the mayonnaise, sour cream, Dijon, and hot sauce. Whisk until thoroughly combined. Serve with the Scotch eggs.

1 pound pork sausage

8 soft-boiled or hard-boiled eggs, peeled

1 large egg

2 tablespoons milk

1 cup crushed pork rinds

SMOKY MUSTARD SAUCE

¼ cup mayonnaise

2 tablespoons sour cream

1 tablespoon Dijon mustard

1 teaspoon chipotle hot sauce

PER SERVING
340 CALORIES
22 G PROTEIN (26%)
1 G CARBS (1%)
28 G FAT (73%)   8 G SAT FAT
0 G FIBER

PORTOBELLO EGGS BENEDICT

MAKES 2 SERVINGS

Traditional Eggs Benedict gets a keto-friendly makeover in the air fryer, and the results couldn't be better! If you really want to intensify the mushroom flavor of this dish, drizzle some truffle oil over the top just before serving.

1 tablespoon olive oil

2 cloves garlic, minced

¼ teaspoon dried thyme

2 portobello mushrooms, stems removed and gills scraped out

2 Roma tomatoes, halved lengthwise

Salt and freshly ground black pepper

2 large eggs

2 tablespoons grated Pecorino Romano cheese

1 tablespoon chopped fresh parsley, for garnish

1 teaspoon truffle oil (optional)

1. Preheat the air fryer to 400°F.

2. In a small bowl, combine the olive oil, garlic, and thyme. Brush the mixture over the mushrooms and tomatoes until thoroughly coated. Season to taste with salt and freshly ground black pepper.

3. Arrange the vegetables, cut side up, in the air fryer basket. Crack an egg into the center of each mushroom and sprinkle with cheese. Air fry for 10 to 14 minutes until the vegetables are tender and the whites are firm. When cool enough to handle, coarsely chop the tomatoes and place on top of the eggs. Scatter parsley on top and drizzle with truffle oil, if desired, just before serving.

PER SERVING
255 CALORIES
11 G PROTEIN (17%)
10 G CARBS (15%)
20 G FAT (68%)   4 G SAT FAT
3 G FIBER

BREAKFAST PIZZA

This dough-from-scratch, restaurant-quality pizza makes an amazing weekend breakfast treat. Packed with flavor, it will fill you with the nutrients you need to rev your metabolism and the energy you need to make the most of the day.

1. Preheat the air fryer to 400°F. Line an 8-inch cake pan with parchment paper and lightly coat the paper with olive oil.

2. In a large bowl, whisk 2 of the eggs with the water, garlic powder, onion powder, and dried oregano. Add the coconut flour, breaking up any lumps with your hands as you add it to the bowl. Stir the coconut flour into the egg mixture, mixing until smooth. Stir in the Parmesan cheese. Allow the mixture to rest for a few minutes until thick and dough-like.

3. Transfer the mixture to the prepared pan. Use a spatula to spread it evenly and slightly up the sides of the pan. Air fry until the crust is set but still light in color, about 10 minutes. Top with the cheeses, sausage, and sun-dried tomatoes.

4. Break the remaining 2 eggs into a small bowl, then slide them onto the pizza. Return the pizza to the air fryer. Air fry 10 to 14 minutes until the egg whites are set and the yolks are the desired doneness. Top with the scallions and allow to rest for 5 minutes before serving.

4 large eggs, divided

1 tablespoon water

½ teaspoon garlic powder

½ teaspoon onion powder

½ teaspoon dried oregano

2 tablespoons coconut flour

3 tablespoons grated Parmesan cheese

½ cup shredded provolone cheese

1 link cooked turkey sausage, chopped (about 2 ounces)

2 sun-dried tomatoes, finely chopped

2 scallions, thinly sliced

PER SERVING
345 CALORIES
29 G PROTEIN (34%)
5 G CARBS (6%)
23 G FAT (60%)   10 G SAT FAT
1 G FIBER

BROCCOLI-MUSHROOM FRITTATA

Frittatas are super easy to cook in an air fryer with less than 5 minutes of prep time, making them ideal for weekend breakfasts as well as light suppers. Feel free to substitute other low-carb vegetables in place of the broccoli if you prefer.

1 tablespoon olive oil

1½ cups broccoli florets, finely chopped

½ cup sliced brown mushrooms

¼ cup finely chopped onion

½ teaspoon salt

¼ teaspoon freshly ground black pepper

6 eggs

¼ cup Parmesan cheese

1. In an 8-inch nonstick cake pan, combine the olive oil, broccoli, mushrooms, onion, salt, and pepper. Stir until the vegetables are thoroughly coated with oil. Place the cake pan in the air fryer basket and set the air fryer to 400°F. Air fry for 5 minutes until the vegetables soften.

2. Meanwhile, in a medium bowl, whisk the eggs and Parmesan until thoroughly combined. Pour the egg mixture into the pan and shake gently to distribute the vegetables. Air fry for another 15 minutes until the eggs are set.

3. Remove from the air fryer and let sit for 5 minutes to cool slightly. Use a silicone spatula to gently lift the frittata onto a plate before serving.

PER SERVING
360 CALORIES
25 G PROTEIN (27%)
10 G CARBS (11%)
25 G FAT (62%)   8 G SAT FAT
2 G FIBER

BACON, CHEESE & AVOCADO MELT

MAKES 2 SERVINGS

Avocados are delicious, nutritious, and keto-compatible. Topped with bacon and melted cheese, they transform into an amazingly satisfying yet simple breakfast. You won't miss that carb-heavy avocado toast once you taste this luscious low-carb dish!

1 avocado

4 slices cooked bacon, chopped

2 tablespoons salsa

1 tablespoon heavy cream

¼ cup shredded Cheddar cheese

1. Preheat the air fryer to 400°F.

2. Slice the avocado in half lengthwise and remove the stone. To ensure the avocado halves do not roll in the basket, slice a thin piece of skin off the base.

3. In a small bowl, combine the bacon, salsa, and cream. Divide the mixture between the avocado halves and top with the cheese.

4. Place the avocado halves in the air fryer basket and air fry for 3 to 5 minutes until the cheese has melted and begins to brown. Serve warm.

PER SERVING
290 CALORIES
11 G PROTEIN (15%)
7 G CARBS (9%)
25 G FAT (76%)   8 G SAT FAT
5 G FIBER

CAJUN BREAKFAST SAUSAGE

MAKES 8 SERVINGS

Fresh, homemade sausage is a keto breakfast treat that reheats beautifully in your air fryer, so consider making a double batch to enjoy throughout the week. If your tastes don't run spicy, simply reduce the amount of Tabasco and cayenne called for in this recipe.

1. Preheat the air fryer to 370°F.

2. In a large bowl, combine the turkey, garlic, onion, Tabasco, Creole seasoning, thyme, paprika, and cayenne. Mix with clean hands until thoroughly combined. Shape into 16 patties, about ½ inch thick. (Wet your hands slightly if you find the sausage too sticky to handle.)

3. Working in batches if necessary, arrange the patties in a single layer in the air fryer basket. Pausing halfway through the cooking time to flip the patties, air fry for 15 to 20 minutes until a thermometer inserted into the thickest portion registers 165°F.

1½ pounds 85% lean ground turkey

3 cloves garlic, finely chopped

¼ onion, grated

1 teaspoon Tabasco sauce

1 teaspoon Creole seasoning

1 teaspoon dried thyme

½ teaspoon paprika

½ teaspoon cayenne

PER SERVING
170 CALORIES
16 G PROTEIN (38%)
1 G CARBS (2%)
11 G FAT (60%) 3 G SAT FAT
0 G FIBER

LEMON-BLUEBERRY MUFFINS

•

Thankfully, muffins aren't off-limits when following a ketogenic eating plan. Simple ingredient swaps help muffins fit into your low-carb day and diet. They cook perfectly in your air fryer with reusable silicone baking cups.

1. Preheat the air fryer to 350°F. Lightly coat 6 silicone muffin cups with vegetable oil. Set aside.

2. In a large mixing bowl, combine the almond flour, Swerve, and baking soda. Set aside.

3. In a separate small bowl, whisk together the eggs, butter, milk, and lemon juice. Add the egg mixture to the flour mixture and stir until just combined. Fold in the blueberries and let the batter sit for 5 minutes.

4. Spoon the muffin batter into the muffin cups, about two-thirds full. Air fry for 20 to 25 minutes, or until a toothpick inserted into the center of a muffin comes out clean.

5. Remove the basket from the air fryer and let the muffins cool for about 5 minutes before transferring them to a wire rack to cool completely.

1¼ cups almond flour

3 tablespoons Swerve sugar replacement

1 teaspoon baking powder

2 large eggs

3 tablespoons melted butter

1 tablespoon milk

1 tablespoon fresh lemon juice

½ cup fresh blueberries

PER MUFFIN
165 CALORIES
10 G PROTEIN (23%)
8 G CARBS (19%)
11 G FAT (58%)   5 G SAT FAT
1 G FIBER

CHICKEN & TURKEY

SOUTHERN FRIED DRUMSTICKS

Crunchy and packed with flavor, these air-fried drumsticks will make you question why you'd ever want to hassle with a deep-fat fryer again. A couple of bags of pork rinds, a great keto-friendly alternative to bread crumbs, will give you more than enough crushed rinds for this recipe.

1 cup buttermilk

2–3 sprigs fresh thyme

1 tablespoon lemon juice

1 teaspoon salt

8 chicken drumsticks, skin on

1½ cups crushed pork rinds

2 teaspoons Old Bay seasoning

1. In a gallon-size resealable bag, combine the buttermilk, thyme, lemon juice, and salt. Add the drumsticks and massage the bag to ensure the chicken is thoroughly coated; refrigerate for 2 hours.

2. Preheat the air fryer to 360°F.

3. In another gallon-size resealable bag, combine the pork rinds and Old Bay seasoning. Working with one or two drumsticks at a time, remove the chicken from the buttermilk mixture and transfer to the bag with the pork rinds. (Discard the marinade.) Seal the bag and shake gently to coat the chicken.

4. Working in batches if necessary, arrange the drumsticks in the air fryer basket, making sure they do not touch. Pausing halfway through the cooking time to turn the chicken, air fry for 20 minutes, or until the skin is browned and a thermometer inserted into the thickest portion registers 165°F.

PER SERVING
500 CALORIES
61 G PROTEIN (50%)
0 G CARBS (0%)
27 G FAT (50%)   8 G SAT FAT
2 G FIBER

EASY CHICKEN FAJITAS

Makes 4 Servings

Skip the carb-heavy tortillas and focus on the most flavorful part of fajitas: the tasty chicken and vegetables inside! You'll hardly miss the tortillas by substituting low-carb lettuce leaves instead. Using prepared guacamole helps you get a fiesta on the table in less than 30 minutes.

1 pound chicken breast tenders, chopped into bite-size pieces

½ onion, thinly sliced

½ red bell pepper, seeded and thinly sliced

½ green bell pepper, seeded and thinly sliced

1 tablespoon vegetable oil

1 tablespoon fajita seasoning

1 teaspoon kosher salt

Juice of ½ lime

8 large lettuce leaves

1 cup prepared guacamole

1. Preheat the air fryer to 400°F.

2. In a large bowl, combine the chicken, onion, and peppers. Drizzle with the vegetable oil and toss until thoroughly coated. Add the fajita seasoning and salt and toss again.

3. Working in batches if necessary, arrange the chicken and vegetables in a single layer in the air fryer basket. Pausing halfway through the cooking time to shake the basket, air fry for 14 minutes, or until the vegetables are tender and a thermometer inserted into the thickest piece of chicken registers 165°F.

4. Transfer the mixture to a serving platter and drizzle with the fresh lime juice. Serve with the lettuce leaves and top with the guacamole.

PER SERVING
400 CALORIES
16 G PROTEIN (15%)
26 G CARBS (25%)
27 G FAT (60%)   5 G SAT FAT
8 G FIBER

COBB SALAD

It's easy to cook bacon and chicken at the same time in an air fryer—just wrap the bacon around the chicken! Paired with a creamy avocado-lime dressing, this Cobb salad reaches a whole new level of flavor.

1. Preheat the air fryer to 400°F.

2. Wrap a piece of bacon around each piece of chicken and secure with a toothpick. Working in batches if necessary, arrange the bacon-wrapped chicken in a single layer in the air fryer basket. Air fry for 8 minutes until the bacon is browned and a thermometer inserted into the thickest piece of chicken register 165°F. Let cool for a few minutes, then slice into bite-size pieces.

3. To make the dressing: In a blender or food processor, combine the yogurt, milk, avocado, lime juice, scallions, garlic, cilantro, and cumin. Puree until smooth. Season to taste with salt and freshly ground pepper.

4. To assemble the salad, in a large bowl, combine the lettuce, tomatoes, and onion. Drizzle the dressing over the vegetables and toss gently until thoroughly combined. Arrange the chicken and eggs on top just before serving.

8 slices reduced-sodium bacon

8 chicken breast tenders (about 1½ pounds)

8 cups chopped romaine lettuce

1 cup cherry tomatoes, halved

¼ red onion, thinly sliced

2 hard-boiled eggs, peeled and sliced

AVOCADO-LIME DRESSING

½ cup plain Greek yogurt

¼ cup milk

½ avocado

Juice of ½ lime

3 scallions, coarsely chopped

1 clove garlic

2 tablespoons fresh cilantro

⅛ teaspoon ground cumin

Salt and freshly ground black pepper

PER SERVING
425 CALORIES
52 G PROTEIN (50%)
11 G CARBS (11%)
18 G FAT (39%) 6 G SAT FAT
4 G FIBER

PERSONAL
CAULIFLOWER PIZZAS

MAKES 2 SERVINGS

Once you get the hang of these low-carb pizzas, you'll find that your air fryer is a great tool for getting a perfectly crispy crust every time. If you'd prefer to make only a single serving, simply refrigerate the unused dough covered in plastic wrap and use within 3 days.

1. Preheat the air fryer to 400°F. Cut 4 sheets of parchment paper to fit the basket of the air fryer. Brush with olive oil and set aside.

2. In a large glass bowl, microwave the cauliflower according to package directions. Place the cauliflower on a clean towel, draw up the sides, and squeeze tightly over a sink to remove the excess moisture. Return the cauliflower to the bowl and add the shredded mozzarella along with the almond flour, Parmesan, egg, salt, garlic powder, and oregano. Stir until thoroughly combined.

3. Divide the dough into two equal portions. Place one piece of dough on the prepared parchment paper and pat gently into a thin, flat disk 7 to 8 inches in diameter. Air fry for 15 minutes until the crust begins to brown. Let cool for 5 minutes.

4. Transfer the parchment paper with the crust on top to a baking sheet. Place a second sheet of parchment paper over the crust. While holding the edges of both sheets together, carefully lift the crust off the baking sheet, flip it, and place it back in the air fryer basket. The new sheet of parchment paper is now on the bottom. Remove the top piece of paper and air fry the crust for another 15 minutes until the top begins to brown. Remove the basket from the air fryer.

5. Spread 2 tablespoons of the marinara sauce on top of the crust, followed by half the fresh mozzarella, chicken, cherry tomatoes, and arugula. Air fry for 5 to 10 minutes longer, until the cheese is melted and beginning to brown. Remove the pizza from the oven and let it sit for 10 minutes before serving. Repeat with the remaining ingredients to make a second pizza.

1 (12-ounce) bag frozen riced cauliflower

⅓ cup shredded mozzarella cheese

¼ cup almond flour

¼ grated Parmesan cheese

1 large egg

½ teaspoon salt

1 teaspoon garlic powder

1 teaspoon dried oregano

4 tablespoons no-sugar-added marinara sauce, divided

4 ounces fresh mozzarella, chopped, divided

1 cup cooked chicken breast, chopped, divided

½ cup chopped cherry tomatoes, divided

¼ cup fresh baby arugula, divided

PER SERVING
550 CALORIES
53 G PROTEIN (46%)
20 G CARBS (17%)
19 G FAT (37 %)   12 G SAT FAT
6 G FIBER

LEMON CHICKEN

Chicken thighs are favored by chefs because they are so tender and flavorful. In this dish you'll find that the delicately roasted chicken skin, which cooks up crisp in your air fryer, is just as delicious and satisfying as the chicken meat.

8 bone-in chicken thighs, skin on

1 tablespoon olive oil

1½ teaspoons lemon-pepper seasoning

½ teaspoon paprika

½ teaspoon garlic powder

¼ teaspoon freshly ground black pepper

Juice of ½ lemon

1. Preheat the air fryer to 360°F.

2. Place the chicken in a large bowl and drizzle with the olive oil. Top with the lemon-pepper seasoning, paprika, garlic powder, and freshly ground black pepper. Toss until thoroughly coated.

3. Working in batches if necessary, arrange the chicken in a single layer in the basket of the air fryer. Pausing halfway through the cooking time to turn the chicken, air fry for 20 to 25 minutes, until a thermometer inserted into the thickest piece registers 165°F.

4. Transfer the chicken to a serving platter and squeeze the lemon juice over the top.

PER SERVING
335 CALORIES
31 G PROTEIN (39%)
0 G CARBS (0%)
22 G FAT (61%)   6 G SAT FAT
0 G FIBER

KEY WEST CHICKEN THIGHS

MAKES 4 SERVINGS

The simplicity of an air fryer makes this recipe a winner when you need to put a hassle-free meal on the table. Marinating your chicken overnight will speed your prep and pack in flavor. For the best browning, be sure to leave a little space between the thighs in the air fryer basket.

1 tablespoon olive oil

Juice of ½ lime

1 tablespoon reduced-sodium soy sauce

1½ teaspoons Montreal chicken seasoning

8 bone-in chicken thighs, skin on

2 tablespoons chopped fresh cilantro

1. In a gallon-size resealable bag, combine the olive oil, lime juice, soy sauce, and chicken seasoning. Add the chicken thighs, seal the bag, and massage the bag to ensure the chicken is thoroughly coated. Refrigerate for at least 2 hours, preferably overnight.

2. Preheat the air fryer to 400°F.

3. Remove the chicken from the marinade (discard the marinade) and arrange in a single layer in the air fryer basket. Pausing halfway through the cooking time to flip the chicken, air fry for 20 to 25 minutes, until a thermometer inserted into the thickest part registers 165°F.

4. Transfer the chicken to a serving platter and top with the cilantro before serving.

PER SERVING
335 CALORIES
31 G PROTEIN (39%)
0 G CARBS (0%)
22 G FAT (61%)   6 G SAT FAT
0 G FIBER

JERK CHICKEN THIGHS

MAKES 6 SERVINGS

While some jerk chicken recipes call for sugar-filled marinades, this version relies on another method: the dry rub. Paired with your air fryer, it's the best way to ensure your chicken achieves a beautifully caramelized coating without resorting to added sugars. If refrigerator space is tight, place the chicken in a resealable bag after you've seasoned it.

1. In a small bowl, combine the coriander, allspice, cayenne, ginger, salt, thyme, cinnamon, and nutmeg. Stir until thoroughly combined.

2. Place the chicken in a 9 x 13-inch baking dish and use paper towels to pat dry. Thoroughly coat both sides of the chicken with the spice mixture. Cover and refrigerate for at least 2 hours, preferably overnight.

3. Preheat the air fryer to 360°F.

4. Working in batches if necessary, arrange the chicken in a single layer in the air fryer basket and lightly coat with the vegetable oil. Pausing halfway through the cooking time to flip the chicken, air fry for 15 to 20 minutes, until a thermometer inserted into the thickest part registers 165°F.

2 teaspoons ground coriander

1 teaspoon ground allspice

1 teaspoon cayenne pepper

1 teaspoon ground ginger

1 teaspoon salt

1 teaspoon dried thyme

½ teaspoon ground cinnamon

½ teaspoon ground nutmeg

2 pounds boneless chicken thighs, skin on

2 tablespoons vegetable oil

PER SERVING
400 CALORIES
35 G PROTEIN (36%)
1 G CARBS (1%)
27 G FAT (63%)   7 G SAT FAT
0 G FIBER

MAKES 4 SERVINGS

Crispy on the outside, juicy on the inside! Did you know you can use an air fryer to make your own amazing rotisserie-style chicken? The secret is in the spice rub that locks in flavor. The circulating hot air ensures the entire chicken gets perfectly browned.

1. Preheat the air fryer to 350°F.

2. Use paper towels to blot the chicken dry. Stuff the chicken with the onion. Rub the chicken with the oil.

3. To make the spice rub: In a small bowl, combine the salt, paprika, onion powder, garlic powder, thyme, black pepper, and cayenne; stir until thoroughly combined. Sprinkle the chicken with the spice rub until thoroughly coated.

4. Place the chicken breast side down in the air fryer basket. Air fry the chicken for 30 minutes. Use tongs to carefully flip the chicken over and air fry for an additional 30 minutes, or until the temperature of a thermometer inserted into the thickest part of the chicken registers 165°F.

5. Let the chicken rest for 10 minutes. Discard the onion and serve.

1 (4-pound) chicken, giblets removed

½ onion, quartered

1 tablespoon vegetable oil

SECRET SPICE RUB

2 teaspoons salt

1 teaspoon paprika

½ teaspoon onion powder

½ teaspoon garlic powder

½ teaspoon dried thyme

½ teaspoon freshly ground black pepper

¼ teaspoon cayenne

PER SERVING
500 CALORIES
61 G PROTEIN (50%)
0 G CARBS (0%)
27 G FAT (50%)   8 G SAT FAT
2 G FIBER

MEDITERRANEAN
STUFFED CHICKEN BREASTS

Loaded with creamy cheese and Mediterranean seasonings, these stuffed chicken breasts make an impressive dish for special occasions. Best of all, they're easy to assemble ahead of time so all you have to do is pop them in the air fryer and prepare a simple sauce before your guests arrive.

4 small boneless, skinless chicken breast halves (about 1½ pounds)

Salt and freshly ground black pepper

4 ounces goat cheese

6 pitted Kalamata olives, coarsely chopped

Zest of ½ lemon

1 teaspoon minced fresh rosemary or ½ teaspoon ground dried rosemary

½ cup almond meal

¼ cup balsamic vinegar

6 tablespoons unsalted butter

1. Preheat the air fryer to 360°F.

2. With a boning knife, cut a wide pocket into the thickest part of each chicken breast half, taking care not to cut all the way through. Season the chicken evenly on both sides with salt and freshly ground black pepper.

3. In a small bowl, mix the cheese, olives, lemon zest, and rosemary. Stuff the pockets with the cheese mixture and secure with toothpicks.

4. Place the almond meal in a shallow bowl and dredge the chicken, shaking off the excess. Coat lightly with olive oil spray.

5. Working in batches if necessary, arrange the chicken breasts in a single layer in the air fryer basket. Pausing halfway through the cooking time to flip the chicken, air fry for 20 to 25 minutes, until a thermometer inserted into the thickest part registers 165°F.

6. While the chicken is baking, prepare the sauce. In a small pan over medium heat, simmer the balsamic vinegar until thick and syrupy, about 5 minutes. Set aside until the chicken is done. When ready to serve, warm the sauce over medium heat and whisk in the butter, 1 tablespoon at a time, until melted and smooth. Season to taste with salt and pepper.

7. Serve the chicken breasts with the sauce drizzled on top.

PER SERVING
510 CALORIES
50 G PROTEIN (39%)
7 G CARBS (5%)
32 G FAT (56%) 18.1 G SAT FAT
0 G FIBER

STUFFED
CHICKEN FLORENTINE

Stuffed chicken cooks up crispy on the outside and tender and delicious on the inside in your air fryer. Keep a bag of frozen spinach leaves on hand for this dish (it's much easier to defrost than spinach sold in blocks). Simply place the spinach leaves in a colander and run warm water over them until defrosted; use a paper towel to ensure you've squeezed out as much water as possible from the spinach before using in this recipe.

1. Place the pine nuts in a small pan and set in the air fryer basket. Set the air fryer to 400°F and air fry for 2 to 3 minutes until toasted. Remove the pine nuts to a mixing bowl and continue preheating the air fryer.

2. In a large bowl, combine the spinach, ricotta, Parmesan, and garlic. Season to taste with salt and pepper and stir well until thoroughly combined.

3. Using a sharp knife, cut into the chicken breasts, slicing them across and opening them up like a book, but be careful not to cut them all the way through. Sprinkle the chicken with salt and pepper.

4. Spoon equal amounts of the spinach mixture into the chicken, then fold the top of the chicken breast back over the top of the stuffing. Wrap each chicken breast with 2 slices of bacon.

5. Working in batches if necessary, air fry the chicken for 18 to 20 minutes until the bacon is crisp and a thermometer inserted into the thickest part of the chicken registers 165°F.

3 tablespoons pine nuts

¾ cup frozen spinach, thawed and squeezed dry

⅓ cup ricotta cheese

2 tablespoons grated Parmesan cheese

3 cloves garlic, minced

Salt and freshly ground black pepper

4 small boneless, skinless chicken breast halves (about 1½ pounds)

8 slices bacon

PER SERVING
440 CALORIES
63 G PROTEIN (56%)
4 G CARBS (4%)
20 G FAT (40%)   6.3 G SAT FAT
1 G FIBER

CHICKEN CROQUETTES
WITH CREOLE SAUCE

MAKES 4 SERVINGS

These keto croquettes are a great way to enjoy any leftover chicken you may have on hand. The almond meal and cheese ensure these patties will be rendered golden and delicious in the air fryer in no time.

2 cups shredded cooked chicken

½ cup shredded Cheddar cheese

2 eggs

¼ cup finely chopped onion

¼ cup almond meal

1 tablespoon poultry seasoning

Vegetable oil

CREOLE SAUCE

¼ cup mayonnaise

¼ cup sour cream

1½ teaspoons Dijon mustard

1½ teaspoons fresh lemon juice

½ teaspoon garlic powder

½ teaspoon Creole seasoning

1. In a large bowl, combine the chicken, Cheddar, eggs, onion, almond meal, and poultry seasoning. Stir gently until thoroughly combined. Cover and refrigerate for 30 minutes.

2. Meanwhile, to make the Creole sauce: In a small bowl, whisk together the mayonnaise, sour cream, Dijon mustard, lemon juice, garlic powder, and Creole seasoning until thoroughly combined. Cover and refrigerate until ready to serve.

3. Preheat the air fryer to 400°F. Divide the chicken mixture into 8 portions and shape into patties.

4. Working in batches if necessary, arrange the patties in a single layer in the air fryer basket and coat both sides lightly with vegetable oil. Pausing halfway through the cooking time to flip the patties, air fry for 10 minutes, or until lightly browned and the cheese is melted. Serve with the Creole sauce.

PER SERVING
380 CALORIES
29 G PROTEIN (30%)
4 G CARBS (4%)
28 G FAT (66%)   8.3 G SAT FAT
0 G FIBER

TANDOORI CHICKEN

The distinct flavor of tandoori chicken is easy to replicate at home, especially with the convenience of an air fryer. And it's a perfect low-carb meal. If you prefer less heat, simply use less cayenne. The dish is often served with basmati rice, but cauliflower "rice" subs in nicely to keep it in the keto zone.

¼ cup plain Greek yogurt

2 cloves garlic, minced

1 tablespoon grated fresh ginger

½ teaspoon ground cayenne

½ teaspoon ground turmeric

½ teaspoon garam masala

1 teaspoon ground cumin

1 teaspoon salt

2 pounds boneless chicken thighs, skin on

2 tablespoons chopped fresh cilantro

1 lemon, cut into 6 wedges

½ sweet onion, sliced

1. In a small bowl, combine the yogurt, garlic, ginger, cayenne, turmeric, garam masala, cumin, and salt. Whisk until thoroughly combined.

2. Transfer the yogurt mixture to a large resealable bag. Add the chicken, seal the bag, and massage the bag to ensure chicken is evenly coated. Refrigerate for 1 hour (or up to 8 hours).

3. Preheat the air fryer to 360°F.

4. Remove the chicken from the marinade (discard the marinade) and arrange in a single layer in the air fryer basket. Pausing halfway through the cooking time to flip the chicken, air fry for 15 to 20 minutes, until a thermometer inserted into the thickest part registers 165°F.

5. Transfer the chicken to a serving platter. Top with the cilantro and serve with the lemon wedges and sliced onion.

PER SERVING
350 CALORIES
35 G PROTEIN (41%)
1 G CARBS (1%)
22 G FAT (58%)   6.2 G SAT FAT
0 G FIBER

CHICKEN CORDON BLEU
CASSEROLE

MAKES 4 SERVINGS

Inspired by the stuffed chicken breast dish filled with ham and creamy Swiss cheese, this recipe borrows all of the same flavors but requires considerably less time to prepare. To keep it keto-friendly, avoid ham with added sugars.

1. Preheat the air fryer to 380°F. Lightly coat a 6-cup casserole dish that will fit in the air fryer, such as an 8-inch round pan, with olive oil and set aside.

2. In a large bowl and using an electric mixer, combine the butter, cream cheese, Dijon mustard, and vinegar. With the motor running on low speed, slowly add the water and beat until smooth. Set aside.

3. Arrange an even layer of chicken in the bottom of the prepared pan, followed by the ham. Spread the butter and cream cheese mixture on top of the ham, followed by the cheese slices on the top layer. Air fry for 20 to 25 minutes until warmed through and the cheese has browned.

¼ cup unsalted butter, softened

4 ounces cream cheese, softened

1½ teaspoons Dijon mustard

2 tablespoons white wine vinegar

¼ cup water

2 cups shredded cooked chicken

¼ pound ham, chopped

4 ounces sliced Swiss or Provolone cheese

PER SERVING
480 CALORIES
34 G PROTEIN (29%)
4 G CARBS (3%)
36 G FAT (68%) 19.7 G SAT FAT
0 G FIBER

CHICKEN AND BROCCOLI
CASEROLE

MAKES 4 SERVINGS

This creamy comfort-food casserole cooks to perfection in your air fryer. A few quick steps in this recipe suggest the use of a microwave for ultimate convenience, but you can certainly use a stovetop if preferred. Serve with a green salad for a keto meal your family will love.

1. Preheat the air fryer to 390°F. Lightly coat a 6-cup casserole dish that will fit in air fryer, such an 8-inch round pan, with olive oil and set aside.

2. Place the broccoli in a large glass bowl with 1 tablespoon of water and cover with a microwavable plate. Microwave on high for 2 to 3 minutes until the broccoli is bright green but not mushy. Drain if necessary and add to another large bowl along with the shredded chicken.

3. In the same glass bowl used to microwave the broccoli, combine the cream cheese and cream. Microwave for 30 seconds to 1 minute on high and stir until smooth. Add the mustard and garlic powder and season to taste with salt and freshly ground black pepper. Whisk until the sauce is smooth.

4. Pour the warm sauce over the broccoli and chicken mixture and then add the basil. Using a silicone spatula, gently fold the mixture until thoroughly combined.

5. Transfer the chicken mixture to the prepared casserole dish and top with the cheese. Air fry for 20 to 25 minutes until warmed through and the cheese has browned.

½ pound broccoli, chopped into florets

2 cups shredded cooked chicken

4 ounces cream cheese

⅓ cup heavy cream

1½ teaspoons Dijon mustard

½ teaspoon garlic powder

Salt and freshly ground black pepper

2 tablespoons chopped fresh basil

1 cup shredded Cheddar cheese

PER SERVING
430 CALORIES
29 G PROTEIN (27%)
6 G CARBS (6%)
32 G FAT (67%)   16.9 G SAT FAT
1 G FIBER

CHICKEN PARMESAN

This classic Italian favorite combines three beloved flavors in one dish: crispy fried chicken, gooey melted cheese, and garlicky marinara sauce. It's a trinity that can't be beat, and it couldn't be easier to make keto-friendly and healthier thanks to the power of an air fryer.

2 large skinless chicken breasts (about 1¼ pounds)

Salt and freshly ground black pepper

½ cup almond meal

½ cup grated Parmesan cheese

2 teaspoons Italian seasoning

1 egg, lightly beaten

1 tablespoon olive oil

1 cup no-sugar-added marinara sauce

4 slices mozzarella cheese or ½ cup shredded mozzarella

1. Preheat the air fryer to 360°F.

2. Slice the chicken breasts in half horizontally to create 4 thinner chicken breasts. Working with one piece at a time, place the chicken between two pieces of parchment paper and pound with a meat mallet or rolling pin to flatten to an even thickness. Season both sides with salt and freshly ground black pepper.

3. In a large shallow bowl, combine the almond meal, Parmesan, and Italian seasoning; stir until thoroughly combined. Place the egg in another large shallow bowl.

4. Dip the chicken in the egg, followed by the almond meal mixture, pressing the mixture firmly into the chicken to create an even coating.

5. Working in batches if necessary, arrange the chicken breasts in a single layer in the air fryer basket and coat both sides lightly with vegetable oil. Pausing halfway through the cooking time to flip the chicken, air fry for 15 minutes, or until a thermometer inserted into the thickest part registers 165°F.

6. Spoon the marinara sauce over each piece of chicken and top with the mozzarella cheese. Air fry for an additional 3 to 5 minutes until the cheese is melted.

PER SERVING
460 CALORIES
65 G PROTEIN (58%)
11 G CARBS (10%)
16 G FAT (32%)   6.4 G SAT FAT
2 G FIBER

TURKEY MEATLOAF

Once you taste how moist meatloaf comes out of your air fryer, you'll never go back to cooking it in a conventional oven. While most large air fryers should have no problem accommodating the size of this meatloaf, you can make smaller loaves if necessary. Just shorten the cooking time.

1. Preheat the air fryer to 350°F. Lightly coat an 8-inch round pan with olive oil and set aside.

2. In a food processor fitted with a metal blade, combine the mushrooms, onion, and garlic. Pulse until finely chopped. Transfer the vegetables to a large mixing bowl.

3. Add the turkey, eggs, tomato paste, almond meal, milk, oregano, salt, and black pepper. Mix gently until thoroughly combined. Transfer the mixture to the prepared pan and shape into a loaf. Arrange the tomato slices on top.

4. Air fry for 50 minutes or until the meatloaf is nicely browned and a thermometer inserted into the thickest part registers 165°F. Remove from the air fryer and let rest for about 10 minutes before slicing.

8 ounces sliced mushrooms

1 small onion, coarsely chopped

2 cloves garlic

1½ pounds 85% lean ground turkey

2 eggs, lightly beaten

1 tablespoon tomato paste

¼ cup almond meal

2 tablespoons milk

1 tablespoon dried oregano

1 teaspoon salt

½ teaspoon freshly ground black pepper

1 Roma tomato, thinly sliced

PER SERVING
420 CALORIES
40 G PROTEIN (37%)
8 G CARBS (8%)
26 G FAT (55%)   6.9 G SAT FAT
1 G FIBER

SIMPLY TERRIFIC
TURKEY MEATBALLS

A food processor makes quick work of preparing these meatballs, which are guaranteed to stay tender and juicy thanks to the fast cooking time an air fryer affords. Enjoy them with spaghetti squash and a sugar-free marinara sauce, or serve them with toothpicks as an irresistible appetizer.

1 red bell pepper, seeded and coarsely chopped

2 cloves garlic, coarsely chopped

¼ cup chopped fresh parsley

1½ pounds 85% lean ground turkey

1 egg, lightly beaten

½ cup grated Parmesan cheese

1 teaspoon salt

½ teaspoon freshly ground black pepper

1. Preheat the air fryer to 400°F.

2. In a food processor fitted with a metal blade, combine the bell pepper, garlic, and parsley. Pulse until finely chopped. Transfer the vegetables to a large mixing bowl.

3. Add the turkey, egg, Parmesan, salt, and black pepper. Mix gently until thoroughly combined. Shape the mixture into 1¼-inch meatballs.

4. Working in batches if necessary, arrange the meatballs in a single layer in the air fryer basket; coat lightly with olive oil spray. Pausing halfway through the cooking time to shake the basket, air fry for 7 to 10 minutes, until lightly browned and a thermometer inserted into the center of a meatball registers 165°F.

PER SERVING
410 CALORIES
38 G PROTEIN (37%)
4 G CARBS (4%)
27 G FAT (59%)   8.2 G SAT FAT
1 G FIBER

BEEF & PORK

POBLANO PEPPER
CHEESEBURGERS

MAKES 4 SERVINGS

Roasting flavorful peppers in the air fryer couldn't be easier. (Poblano peppers provide a little heat but much less than the typical jalapeño.) The beef burgers also cook up super juicy in your air fryer! To keep this recipe keto-friendly, use lettuce leaves in place of traditional hamburger buns.

2 poblano chile peppers

1½ pounds 85% lean ground beef

1 clove garlic, minced

1 teaspoon salt

½ teaspoon freshly ground black pepper

4 slices Cheddar cheese (about 3 ounces)

4 large lettuce leaves

1. Preheat the air fryer to 400°F.

2. Arrange the poblano peppers in the basket of the air fryer. Pausing halfway through the cooking time to turn the peppers, air fry for 20 minutes, or until they are softened and beginning to char. Transfer the peppers to a large bowl and cover with a plate. When cool enough to handle, peel off the skin, remove the seeds and stems, and slice into strips. Set aside.

3. Meanwhile, in a large bowl, combine the ground beef with the garlic, salt, and pepper. Shape the beef into 4 patties.

4. Lower the heat on the air fryer to 360°F. Arrange the burgers in a single layer in the basket of the air fryer. Pausing halfway through the cooking time to turn the burgers, air fry for 10 minutes, or until a thermometer inserted into the thickest part registers 160°F.

5. Top the burgers with the cheese slices and continue baking for a minute or two, just until the cheese has melted. Serve the burgers on a lettuce leaf topped with the roasted poblano peppers.

PER SERVING
310 CALORIES
28 G PROTEIN (37%)
3 G CARBS (4%)
20 G FAT (59%)   9.2 G SAT FAT
1 G FIBER

CHEESEBURGER CASSEROLE

This casserole is the ultimate comfort food and combines the classic flavors of a cheeseburger in one delicious dish. Best of all, you can use your air fryer to put everything together in a snap. And with only 8 carbs per serving, it definitely qualifies as keto-friendly cuisine.

1. Lightly coat a 6-cup casserole dish that will fit in air fryer, such an 8-inch round pan, with olive oil and set aside.

2. Arrange the bacon in a single layer in the air fryer basket (it's OK if the bacon sits a bit on the sides). Set the air fryer to 350°F and air fry for 10 minutes. Check for crispiness and air fry for 2 to 3 minutes longer if needed. Transfer the bacon to a plate lined with paper towels and let cool. Drain the grease.

3. Set the air fryer to 400°F. Crumble the beef into a single layer in the air fryer basket. Scatter the garlic on top and sprinkle with the onion powder. Air fry for 15 to 20 minutes until the beef is browned and cooked through.

4. While the beef is baking, in a bowl whisk together the eggs, cream, tomato paste, pickle relish, salt, and pepper. Stir in 1 cup of the cheese. Set aside.

5. When the beef is done, transfer it to the prepared pan. Use the side of a spoon to break up any large pieces of beef.

6. Drain the grease and, when cool enough to handle, wash the air fryer basket. Set the air fryer to 350°F.

7. Crumble the bacon and add it to the beef, spreading the meats into an even layer. Pour the egg mixture over the beef mixture and top with the remaining ½ cup of cheese. Air fry for 20 to 25 minutes until the eggs are set and the top is golden brown.

¼ pound reduced-sodium bacon

1 pound 85% lean ground beef

1 clove garlic, minced

¼ teaspoon onion powder

4 eggs

¼ cup heavy cream

¼ cup tomato paste

2 tablespoons dill pickle relish

¼ teaspoon salt

¼ teaspoon freshly ground black pepper

1½ cups grated Cheddar cheese, divided

PER SERVING
660 CALORIES
50 G PROTEIN (30%)
8 G CARBS (5%)
47 G FAT (65%)   20.4 G SAT FAT
1 G FIBER

STUFFED PEPPERS

Browning ground beef in your air fryer keeps this recipe super simple—and no more grease splatters on your stovetop! Meanwhile, a few minutes in the microwave gives your bell peppers a valuable head start on cooking. Then all the flavors come back together in your air fryer with a cheesy finishing touch your family will love.

1 pound 85% lean ground beef

½ yellow onion, chopped

4 bell peppers, tops and seeds removed

1 (10-ounce) package cauliflower "rice," fresh or frozen

½ cup tomato sauce

2 tablespoons chopped fresh parsley

1 teaspoon salt

½ teaspoon freshly ground black pepper

1 cup shredded Cheddar cheese

1 teaspoon fresh chopped dill or parsley, for garnish (optional)

1. Preheat the air fryer to 400°F.

2. Crumble the beef into a single layer in the air fryer basket. Scatter the onion on top. Air fry for 15 to 20 minutes until the beef is browned and cooked through. Lower the air fryer to 360°F.

3. Meanwhile, arrange the bell peppers in a microwave-safe dish and cover loosely with parchment paper or plastic wrap. Microwave on high for 2 to 3 minutes until the peppers begin to soften.

4. To assemble the peppers, carefully transfer the beef and onions to a large mixing bowl. Use the side of a spoon to break up any large pieces of beef. Drain the grease and wash the air fryer basket.

5. To the beef mixture add the cauliflower "rice," tomato sauce, parsley, salt, and black pepper. Stir gently until thoroughly combined.

6. Divide the mixture among the peppers and arrange cut-side up in the air fryer basket. Air fry for 15 to 20 minutes until the peppers are soft. Top with the cheese and air fry for 1 to 2 minutes longer until melted. Garnish with herbs if desired.

PER SERVING

380 CALORIES

32 G PROTEIN (33%)

13 G CARBS (13%)

23 G FAT (54%)   10.6 G SAT FAT

4 G FIBER

STEAK SALAD
WITH SMOKY BLUE CHEESE DRESSING

MAKES 4 SERVINGS

Consider this salad a feast on a plate! And with only 12 grams of carbohydrate per serving, it's a very keto-friendly meal. For best results, let the steak sit at room temperature for about half an hour before taking it to your air fryer.

1 pound sirloin steak

1 tablespoon steak seasoning

8 cups chopped romaine lettuce

2 avocados, peeled, pitted, and sliced

½ cup cherry tomatoes, halved

¼ red onion, thinly sliced

¼ cup crumbled blue cheese

SMOKY BLUE CHEESE DRESSING

½ cup mayonnaise

¼ cup buttermilk

1 tablespoon chipotle hot sauce

1 teaspoon garlic powder

½ teaspoon Worcestershire sauce

¼ cup crumbled blue cheese

Salt and freshly ground black pepper

1. Preheat the air fryer to 400°F.

2. Rub the steak with the steak seasoning. Arrange the steak in the air fryer basket and spray lightly with olive oil. Pausing halfway through the cooking time to turn the meat, air fry for 12 to 15 minutes, until a thermometer inserted into the thickest part indicates the desired doneness, 125°F (rare) or 150°F (medium). Let the steaks rest for 10 minutes before slicing into bite-size pieces.

3. Meanwhile, to make the dressing: In a bowl, combine the mayonnaise, buttermilk, hot sauce, garlic powder, and Worcestershire sauce. Whisk until smooth. Stir in the blue cheese and season to taste with salt and freshly ground black pepper.

4. To assemble the salad, place the lettuce on the bottom of the plate or serving bowl. Top with the avocado slices, tomatoes, and red onion, followed by the steak slices. Scatter the blue cheese crumbles on top and serve with the dressing on the side.

PER SERVING
610 CALORIES
28 G PROTEIN (18%)
12 G CARBS (8%)
51 G FAT (74%)   12.8 SAT FAT
7 G FIBER

MARINATED STEAK TIPS
WITH MUSHROOMS

Makes 4 Servings

You might be talking about the delicious results for weeks, but it takes just a few minutes to put this recipe together. Let the marinade do its magic and your air fryer will take care of the rest, so you can have this juicy steak dinner on the table fast!

1. Place the beef and mushrooms in a gallon-size resealable bag. In a small bowl, whisk together the Worcestershire, mustard, olive oil, paprika, and red pepper flakes. Pour the marinade into the bag and massage gently to ensure the beef and mushrooms are evenly coated. Seal the bag and refrigerate for at least 4 hours, preferably overnight. Remove from the refrigerator 30 minutes before cooking.

2. Preheat the air fryer to 400°F.

3. Drain and discard the marinade. Arrange the steak and mushrooms in the air fryer basket. Air fry for 10 minutes, pausing halfway through the baking time to shake the basket. Transfer to a serving plate and top with the parsley, if desired.

1½ pounds sirloin, trimmed and cut into 1-inch pieces

8 ounces brown mushrooms, halved

¼ cup Worcestershire sauce

1 tablespoon Dijon mustard

1 tablespoon olive oil

1 teaspoon paprika

1 teaspoon crushed red pepper flakes

2 tablespoons chopped fresh parsley (optional)

PER SERVING
330 CALORIES
41 G PROTEIN (51%)
2 G CARBS (2%)
17 G FAT (47%)   6.2 G SAT FAT
0 G FIBER

THAI BEEF SATAY
WITH PEANUT SAUCE

MAKES 4 SERVINGS

Forget the preheating and managing a grill! Prep ahead and you can have these mouthwatering skewers ready to savor in just 2 to 3 minutes of air-frying time. You'll need small metal skewers that fit into your air fryer or bamboo skewers that have been soaked in water for an hour before using.

Juice of 3 limes

½ cup fresh cilantro

4 cloves garlic

1-inch piece fresh ginger, peeled and chopped

2 tablespoons Swerve sugar replacement

2 tablespoons fish sauce

2 tablespoons reduced-sodium soy sauce

1 teaspoon sriracha or chili-garlic sauce

2 teaspoons sesame oil

1½ pounds flank steak, sliced ¼ inch thick against the grain

2 medium cucumbers, peeled and sliced

PEANUT SAUCE

½ cup creamy peanut butter

Juice of ½ lime

1 tablespoon reduced-sodium soy sauce

1 teaspoon Swerve sugar replacement

1 teaspoon grated fresh ginger

1 teaspoon chili-garlic sauce

⅓ cup water

1. In a food processor or blender, puree the lime juice, cilantro, garlic, ginger, Swerve, fish sauce, soy sauce, sriracha, and sesame oil.

2. Place the steak slices into a gallon-size resealable bag and pour the marinade over the top of the meat. Seal the bag and refrigerate for at least an hour or up to 4 hours.

3. To make the peanut sauce: In a medium bowl, combine the peanut butter, lime juice, soy sauce, Swerve, ginger, and chili-garlic sauce. Slowly add the water and whisk until smooth. Cover and refrigerate until ready to serve.

4. Preheat the air fryer to 400°F.

5. Discard the marinade and thread the meat slices back and forth onto skewers. Working in batches if necessary, air fry the satay skewers for 2 or 3 minutes until cooked through, pausing halfway through the time to turn the skewers. Serve with the peanut sauce and the cucumbers.

PER SERVING
480 CALORIES
34 G PROTEIN (28%)
9 G CARBS (8%)
34 G FAT (64%)   10.2 G SAT FAT
2 G FIBER

LONDON BROIL
WITH HERB BUTTER

London broil benefits from a long marinating time, but if you prep ahead, the magic can happen in your fridge overnight. Then treating your meat to the even hot-air circulation of the air fryer will bring even greater tenderizing. Remember to always let your meat rest for 10 minutes before slicing, and make sure to slice against the grain for best results.

1½ pounds London broil top round steak

¼ cup olive oil

2 tablespoons balsamic vinegar

1 tablespoon Worcestershire sauce

4 cloves garlic, minced

HERB BUTTER

6 tablespoons unsalted butter, softened

1 tablespoon chopped fresh parsley

¼ teaspoon salt

¼ teaspoon dried ground rosemary or thyme

¼ teaspoon garlic powder

Pinch of red pepper flakes

1. Place the beef in a gallon-size resealable bag. In a small bowl, whisk together the olive oil, balsamic vinegar, Worcestershire sauce, and garlic. Pour the marinade over the beef, massaging gently to coat, and seal the bag. Let sit at room temperature for an hour or refrigerate overnight.

2. To make the herb butter: In a small bowl, mix the butter with the parsley, salt, rosemary, garlic powder, and red pepper flakes until smooth. Cover and refrigerate until ready to use.

3. Preheat the air fryer to 400°F.

4. Remove the beef from the marinade (discard the marinade) and place the beef in the air fryer basket. Pausing halfway through the cooking time to turn the meat, air fry for 20 to 25 minutes, until a thermometer inserted into the thickest part indicates the desired doneness, 125°F (rare) to 150°F (medium). Let the beef rest for 10 minutes before slicing. Serve topped with the herb butter.

PER SERVING
420 CALORIES
41 G PROTEIN (39%)
1 G CARBS (1%)
28 G FAT (60%)   13.8 G SAT FAT
0 G FIBER

ROAST BEEF
WITH HORSERADISH CREAM

MAKES 6 SERVINGS

Here's your solution to Sunday dinner. A classic beef roast stays so tender without any fuss when it cooks in your air fryer. And the horseradish cream is a heavenly keto treat! If you're lucky, you'll have some leftovers to enjoy in a salad later in the week.

1. Preheat the air fryer to 400°F.

2. Season the beef with the salt, garlic powder, black pepper, and thyme. Place the beef fat-side down in the basket of the air fryer and lightly coat with olive oil. Pausing halfway through the cooking time to turn the meat, air fry for 35 to 45 minutes, until a thermometer inserted into the thickest part indicates the desired doneness, 125°F (rare) to 150°F (medium). Let the beef rest for 10 minutes before slicing.

3. To make the horseradish cream: In a small bowl, combine the heavy cream, sour cream, horseradish, and lemon juice. Whisk until thoroughly combined. Season to taste with salt and freshly ground black pepper. Serve alongside the beef.

2 pounds beef roast top round or eye of round

1 tablespoon salt

2 teaspoons garlic powder

1 teaspoon freshly ground black pepper

1 teaspoon dried thyme

HORSERADISH CREAM

⅓ cup heavy cream

⅓ cup sour cream

⅓ cup prepared horseradish

2 teaspoons fresh lemon juice

Salt and freshly ground black pepper

PER SERVING
280 CALORIES
34 G PROTEIN (51%)
3 G CARBS (5%)
13 G FAT (44%)   6.6 G SAT FAT
1 G FIBER

GREEK MEATBALLS
WITH TZATZIKI SAUCE

MAKES 4 SERVINGS

These flavorful meatballs with their creamy sauce elevate ground beef to a whole new level and are guaranteed to become a family favorite. Serve with a simple Greek salad on the side for a complete meal. For an appetizer version, make the meatballs slightly smaller and adjust the cooking time accordingly.

1. Preheat the air fryer to 350°F.

2. In a large mixing bowl, combine the beef, zucchini, feta, red onion, garlic powder, oregano, salt, black pepper, and lemon juice. Mix gently until thoroughly combined. Shape the mixture into 1¼-inch meatballs.

3. Working in batches if necessary, arrange the meatballs in a single layer in the air fryer basket; coat lightly with olive oil spray. Pausing halfway through the cooking time to shake the basket, air fry for 10 to 15 minutes, until the meatballs are browned and a thermometer inserted into the center of a meatball registers 160°F.

4. To make the tzatziki sauce: In a bowl, combine the sour cream, cucumber, lemon juice, garlic powder, dill, salt, and black pepper. Stir until thoroughly combined. Serve with the meatballs.

1 pound 85% lean ground beef

1 cup grated zucchini

½ cup crumbled feta cheese

2 tablespoons finely minced red onion

1 teaspoon garlic powder

1 teaspoon dried oregano

1 teaspoon salt

½ teaspoon freshly ground black pepper

2 teaspoons fresh lemon juice

TZATZIKI SAUCE

½ cup sour cream

¼ cup grated cucumber

1 tablespoon fresh lemon juice

½ teaspoon garlic powder

½ teaspoon dried dill

½ teaspoon salt

½ teaspoon freshly ground black pepper

PER SERVING
330 CALORIES
26 G PROTEIN (32%)
4 G CARBS (5%)
23 G FAT (63%)   11.1 G SAT FAT
1 G FIBER

CHICKEN FRIED STEAK
WITH CREAM GRAVY

MAKES 4 SERVINGS

Here's a beloved Southern dish you're unlikely to see in any other type of weight loss eating plan, but it's a feasible treat on a ketogenic diet with a few strategic ingredient swaps. Take care in handling the cube steaks; the pork rind coating is far more delicate than a traditional flour-based crust.

4 small thin cube steaks (about 1 pound)

½ teaspoon salt

½ teaspoon freshly ground black pepper

¼ teaspoon garlic powder

1 egg, lightly beaten

1 cup crushed pork rinds (about 3 ounces)

CREAM GRAVY

½ cup heavy cream

2 ounces cream cheese

¼ cup bacon grease

2–3 tablespoons water

2–3 dashes Worcestershire sauce

Salt and freshly ground black pepper

1. Preheat the air fryer to 400°F.

2. Working one at a time, place the steak between two sheets of parchment paper and use a meat mallet to pound to an even thickness.

3. In a small bowl, combine the salt, pepper, and garlic power. Season both sides of each steak with the mixture.

4. Place the egg in a small shallow dish and the pork rinds in another small shallow dish. Dip each steak first in the egg wash, followed by the pork rinds, pressing lightly to form an even coating. Working in batches if necessary, arrange the steaks in a single layer in the air fryer basket. Air fry for 10 minutes until crispy and cooked through.

5. To make the cream gravy: In a heavy-bottomed pot, warm the cream, cream cheese, and bacon grease over medium heat, whisking until smooth. Lower the heat if the mixture begins to boil. Continue whisking as you slowly add the water, 1 tablespoon at a time, until the sauce reaches the desired consistency. Season with the Worcestershire sauce and salt and pepper to taste. Serve over the chicken fried steaks.

PER SERVING
560 CALORIES
43 G PROTEIN (31%)
2 G CARBS (1%)
42 G FAT (68%)   19.1 G SAT FAT
0 G FIBER

ITALIAN-STYLE PORK CHOPS

While these pork chops are guaranteed to stay moist and delicious, the tomatoes will thicken nicely into a sauce through the magic of air frying. Serve over spiralized zucchini "noodles" for a satisfying Italian dinner that will taste like you spent far longer in the kitchen than you really did.

1. Preheat the air fryer to 400°F.

2. Arrange the pork chops in a round 8-inch baking dish. Drizzle with the olive oil and season both sides with the salt.

3. In a bowl, combine the tomatoes, Italian seasoning, and garlic. Pour the tomato mixture over the pork chops.

4. Pausing halfway through the cooking time to turn the chops, air fry for 20 to 25 minutes, until a thermometer inserted into the thickest piece registers 145°F. Remove the chops from the sauce and let rest for 5 minutes. Stir the olives and parsley into the sauce before serving with the pork chops.

4 thick center-cut boneless pork chops (about 1½ pounds)

1 tablespoon olive oil

1 teaspoon salt

1 (15-ounce) can crushed tomatoes

1 tablespoon Italian seasoning

2 cloves garlic, minced

¼ cup chopped kalamata olives

2 tablespoons chopped fresh parsley

PER SERVING
350 CALORIES
40 G PROTEIN (46%)
9 G CARBS (10%)
17 G FAT (44%) 5.2 G SAT FAT
2 G FIBER

CRISPY PORK CHOPS

MAKES 4 SERVINGS

Pork rinds and Parmesan cheese form the perfect keto-friendly crust for these juicy pork chops. A simple buttermilk marinade makes them extra tender and delicious. However, if you're pressed for time, feel free to skip that step.

4 thick center-cut boneless pork chops (about 1½ pounds)

1 cup buttermilk

1 cup crushed pork rinds

¼ cup grated Parmesan cheese

1 teaspoon smoked paprika

½ teaspoon onion powder

½ teaspoon chili powder

1 large egg

½ teaspoon salt

¼ teaspoon freshly ground black pepper

1. In a gallon-size resealable bag, combine the pork chops and buttermilk. Seal the bag and massage the meat to coat with the buttermilk. Refrigerate for at least 2 hours, preferably overnight.

2. Preheat the air fryer to 400°F.

3. In a shallow bowl, combine the pork rinds, Parmesan, paprika, onion powder, and chili powder. In a separate shallow bowl, lightly beat the egg.

4. Remove the pork chops from the buttermilk marinade (discard the marinade). Season both sides of each pork chop with the salt and freshly ground black pepper. Working one at a time, dip each pork chop in the egg, followed by the pork rind mixture, pressing lightly to form an even coating.

5. Working in batches if necessary, arrange the chops in a single layer in the air fryer basket. Pausing halfway through the cooking time to turn the chops, air fry for 12 to 15 minutes, until crispy and a thermometer inserted into the thickest piece registers 145°F. Let rest for 5 minutes before serving.

PER SERVING
430 CALORIES
54 G PROTEIN (52%)
1 G CARBS (1%)
22 G FAT (47%)   8.1 G SAT FAT
0 G FIBER

ITALIAN SAUSAGES
WITH PEPPERS AND MUSHROOMS

Sausages and peppers are a classic combination. However, a bit of mozzarella really brings the ingredients together in a delightful way and improves the keto profile. Enjoy this dish with a fresh garden salad and spiralized zucchini "noodles."

8 ounces sliced brown mushrooms

1 red bell pepper, seeded and cut into thick strips

1 green bell pepper, seeded and cut into thick strips

1 tablespoon olive oil

½ teaspoon salt

½ teaspoon Italian seasoning

4 hot or mild pork Italian sausage links (about 1 pound)

1 cup grated mozzarella cheese

1. Preheat the air fryer to 380°F. Coat an 8-inch round baking dish with olive oil and set aside.

2. In a large bowl, combine the mushrooms, peppers, olive oil, salt, and Italian seasoning. Toss until thoroughly coated. Transfer the vegetable mixture to the basket of the air fryer and arrange the sausages on top.

3. Pausing halfway through the cooking time to turn the sausages and toss the vegetables, air fry for 15 to 20 minutes, until the vegetables are tender and beginning to brown and a thermometer inserted into the sausage registers 160°F. Top with the cheese and air fry for 2 to 3 minutes longer until the cheese is melted.

PER SERVING
440 CALORIES
24 G PROTEIN (22%)
10 G CARBS (9%)
34 G FAT (69%)   13.1 G SAT FAT
1 G FIBER

KIELBASA AND CABBAGE

One bowl of low-carb ingredients can go straight to your air fryer for amazing results! Adding a little water to the air fryer basket helps the cabbage steam as it cooks. Then a few shakes of the basket is all the dish requires. Use tongs to toss the cabbage if you find it easier than shaking.

1. Preheat the air fryer to 400°F.

2. In a large bowl, combine the sausage, cabbage, onion, garlic, olive oil, salt, and black pepper. Toss until thoroughly combined.

3. Transfer the mixture to the basket of the air fryer and pour the water over the top. Pausing two or three times during the cooking time to shake the basket, air fry for 20 to 25 minutes, until the sausage is browned and the vegetables are tender.

1 pound smoked kielbasa sausage, sliced into ½-inch pieces

1 head cabbage, very coarsely chopped

½ yellow onion, chopped

2 cloves garlic, chopped

2 tablespoons olive oil

½ teaspoon salt

½ teaspoon freshly ground black pepper

¼ cup water

PER SERVING
410 CALORIES
14 G PROTEIN (13%)
19 G CARBS (18%)
32 G FAT (69%)   9.4 G SAT FAT
6 G FIBER

CHINESE-STYLE SPARERIBS

Who needs takeout when you can make your own finger-licking-good ribs in the air fryer? Save the cost and control the nutritional profile by keeping your ribs in the keto zone right at home. The longer the meat marinates, the more flavorful the results.

1. In a small bowl, combine the sesame oil, black bean paste, rice vinegar, soy sauce, Swerve, garlic, and ginger. Stir until thoroughly combined. Transfer the marinade to a gallon-size resealable bag and add the ribs. Seal the bag and massage the ribs to coat with the marinade. Refrigerate for at least 4 hours, preferably overnight.

2. Preheat the air fryer to 380°F.

3. Working in batches if necessary, arrange the ribs in a single layer in the basket of the air fryer. Pausing halfway through the cooking time to turn the ribs, air fry for 30 to 35 minutes, until tender and browned.

1 tablespoon sesame oil

1 tablespoon fermented black bean paste

1 tablespoon seasoned rice vinegar

1 tablespoon reduced-sodium soy sauce

1 tablespoon Swerve sugar replacement

1 teaspoon minced garlic

1 teaspoon grated fresh ginger

2 pounds pork spareribs, cut into small pieces

PER SERVING
380 CALORIES
26 G PROTEIN (28%)
0 G CARBS (0%)
30 G FAT (72%)   10.2 G SAT FAT
0 G FIBER

THAI PORK MEATBALLS

These Asian-style meatballs are hearty and satisfying, as well as quite easy to prepare with low-carb ingredients. You can easily reheat leftovers using your air fryer, and then add them to lettuce wrap sandwiches, soups, or salads.

1 small zucchini, shredded

¾ teaspoon salt, divided

2 pounds 84% lean ground pork

2 eggs

½ cup blanched almond flour

¼ cup chopped fresh cilantro

2 tablespoons fish sauce

2 large jalapeños, seeded and finely chopped

2 cloves garlic, minced

2 scallions, sliced

1 teaspoon grated fresh ginger

Zest of 1 lime

1 teaspoon sesame seeds, for garnish

1. Place the zucchini in a colander in the sink or over a large bowl. Sprinkle with ¼ teaspoon of the salt and let drain for 15 to 30 minutes. Squeeze out as much moisture as possible and then place the zucchini in a large bowl. Add the remaining ½ teaspoon salt, pork, eggs, almond flour, cilantro, fish sauce, jalapeños, garlic, scallions, ginger, and lime zest. Shape the meat mixture into 1¼-inch meatballs.

2. Preheat the air fryer to 380°F.

3. Working in batches if necessary, arrange the meatballs in a single layer in the air fryer basket; coat lightly with olive oil spray. Pausing halfway through the cooking time to shake the basket, air fry for 7 to 10 minutes, until lightly browned and a thermometer inserted into the center of a meatball registers 160°F. Garnish with sesame seeds before serving.

PER SERVING
340 CALORIES
29 G PROTEIN (34%)
5 G CARBS (6%)
23 G FAT (60%)   6.9 G SAT FAT
1 G FIBER

VIETNAMESE PORK SALAD

The pork crispy from your air fryer is the star of the dish! This style of Asian salad is traditionally served with rice noodles, but you can make this dish keto-friendly by enjoying it with spiralized raw cucumber "noodles" instead. If you don't have a spiralizer, seed and thinly slice the cucumbers.

1. In a large glass bowl, whisk together the onion, garlic, soy sauce, oil, Swerve, fish sauce, lemongrass paste, and pepper.

2. Add the pork to the marinade and refrigerate, covered, for 1 hour or up to 24 hours.

3. Preheat the air fryer to 400°F.

4. Working in batches if necessary, remove the pork from the marinade (discard the marinade) and arrange the pork in a single layer in the air fryer basket. Pausing halfway through the cooking time to shake the basket, air fry for 7 to 10 minutes, until the pork is cooked through and the edges are browned.

5. To assemble the salad, place the cucumber spirals on a serving dish and top with the pork; scatter the roasted peanuts and cilantro on top. Serve with the lime wedges.

¼ cup minced onion

3 cloves garlic, minced

2 tablespoons reduced-sodium soy sauce

2 tablespoons vegetable oil

1 tablespoon Swerve sugar replacement

1 tablespoon fish sauce

1 tablespoon minced lemongrass paste

½ teaspoon freshly ground black pepper

1 pound boneless pork chops, sliced into ¼-inch strips

2 large cucumbers, peeled and spiralized

¼ cup crushed roasted peanuts

2 tablespoons chopped fresh cilantro

1 lime, cut into wedges

PER SERVING
310 CALORIES
29 G PROTEIN (37%)
6 G CARBS (8%)
19 G FAT (55%)   4.4 SAT FAT
2 G FIBER

FISH & SEAFOOD

CRAB CAKES
WITH LEMON AIOLI

MAKES 4 SERVINGS

These crab cakes brown so nicely in your air fryer. And they shine when paired with the light and lemony mayonnaise sauce. Everyone who tries a taste—following a keto diet or not—will discover a new favorite meal!

2 (8-ounce) cans crabmeat, drained and picked over to remove any bits of shell

2 eggs

¼ cup almond flour

3 tablespoons mayonnaise

1 tablespoon Dijon mustard

1 teaspoon Old Bay seasoning

1 tablespoon chopped fresh parsley

½ teaspoon salt

LEMON AIOLI

¼ cup mayonnaise

2 teaspoons fresh lemon juice

1 teaspoon Dijon mustard

½ teaspoon garlic powder

½ teaspoon Old Bay seasoning

1. Preheat the air fryer to 350°F. Line the basket with parchment paper.

2. In a large bowl, combine the crabmeat, eggs, almond flour, mayonnaise, Dijon mustard, Old Bay seasoning, parsley, and salt. Use a silicone spatula to gently fold until thoroughly combined, taking care not to break up the crabmeat too much.

3. Use an ice cream scoop to form the crab mixture patties. Place in a single layer on the lined air fryer basket, then press lightly with the bottom of the scoop to flatten the patties into a circle about ½ inch thick. Pausing halfway through the cooking time to turn the patties, air fry for 10 minutes until lightly browned.

4. To make the lemon aioli: In a small bowl, combine the mayonnaise, lemon juice, Dijon mustard, garlic powder, and Old Bay seasoning. Stir until thoroughly combined.

5. Serve the crab cakes topped with the aioli sauce.

PER SERVING
350 CALORIES
26 G PROTEIN (30%)
3 G CARBS (3%)
26 G FAT (67%) 3.8 G SAT FAT
1 G FIBER

BBQ SHRIMP
WITH CREOLE BUTTER SAUCE

The Worcestershire-spiked butter sauce makes this New Orleans–style shrimp dish over-the-top delicious. Your air fryer knows just what to do to produce perfect shrimp that's not overcooked. Serve with cauliflower "rice" to help soak up every last bit of the sauce.

6 tablespoons unsalted butter

⅓ cup Worcestershire sauce

3 cloves garlic, minced

Juice of 1 lemon

1 teaspoon paprika

1 teaspoon Creole seasoning

1½ pounds large uncooked shrimp, peeled and deveined

2 tablespoons fresh parsley

1. Preheat the air fryer to 370°F.

2. In a large microwave-safe bowl, combine the butter, Worcestershire, and garlic. Microwave on high for 1 to 2 minutes until the butter is melted. Stir in the lemon juice, paprika, and Creole seasoning. Add the shrimp and toss until thoroughly coated.

3. Transfer the mixture to a casserole dish or pan that fits in your air fryer. Pausing halfway through the cooking time to turn the shrimp, air fry for 12 to 15 minutes, until the shrimp are cooked through. Top with the parsley just before serving.

PER SERVING
300 CALORIES
24 G PROTEIN (32%)
8 G CARBS (11%)
19 G FAT (57%)   11.4 G SAT FAT
0 G FIBER

SPANISH SHRIMP KEBABS

Keto never needs to be boring! Spice up any dinner with these skewers big on flavor but easy on time and ingredients required. Use smoked chorizo, which will be firm because it has already been cooked. You'll need small metal skewers that fit into your air fryer for this recipe. If you prefer bamboo skewers, be sure to soak them in water for an hour before using.

1. Preheat the air fryer to 400°F.

2. In a large bowl, combine the shrimp, bell pepper, olive oil, paprika, salt, and garlic. Toss gently until thoroughly coated.

3. Thread the shrimp, peppers, and sausage onto the skewers, alternating ingredients as you go.

4. Working in batches if necessary and pausing halfway through the cooking time to turn the skewers, air fry the skewers for 12 to 15 minutes, until the peppers are tender and the shrimp are cooked through.

1½ pounds large shrimp, peeled and deveined

1 large bell pepper, seeded and chopped into 1-inch pieces

2 tablespoons olive oil

1 teaspoon smoked paprika

¾ teaspoon salt

3 cloves garlic, minced

8 ounces smoked chorizo, sliced into ½-inch rounds

PER SERVING
450 CALORIES
38 G PROTEIN (34%)
6 G CARBS (5%)
30 G FAT (61%)   9.5 G SAT FAT
1 G FIBER

COCONUT SHRIMP
WITH SPICY DIPPING SAUCE

MAKES 4 SERVINGS

You may not consider shrimp, coconut, and pork rinds to be obvious ingredients that go together, but in this recipe they work beautifully. The shrimp stays especially nice and juicy because of the crisp outer coating, and the coconut flavor really comes through (without the need to resort to sweetened flakes) because of the coconut flour.

1. Preheat the air fryer to 390°F.

2. In a food processor fitted with a metal blade, combine the pork rinds and coconut flakes. Pulse until the mixture resembles coarse crumbs. Transfer to a shallow bowl.

3. In another shallow bowl, combine the coconut flour, onion powder, and garlic powder; mix until thoroughly combined.

4. In a third shallow bowl, whisk the eggs until slightly frothy.

5. In a large bowl, season the shrimp with the salt and pepper, tossing gently to coat.

6. Working a few pieces at a time, dredge the shrimp in the flour mixture, followed by the eggs, and finishing with the pork rind crumb mixture. Arrange the shrimp on a baking sheet until ready to air fry.

7. Working in batches if necessary, arrange the shrimp in a single layer in the air fryer basket. Pausing halfway through the cooking time to turn the shrimp, air fry for 8 minutes until cooked through.

8. To make the sauce: In a small bowl, combine the mayonnaise, sriracha, lime zest and juice, and garlic. Whisk until thoroughly combined. Serve alongside the shrimp.

1 (2½-ounce) bag pork rinds

¾ cup unsweetened shredded coconut flakes

¾ cup coconut flour

1 teaspoon onion powder

1 teaspoon garlic powder

2 eggs

1½ pounds large shrimp, peeled and deveined

½ teaspoon salt

¼ teaspoon freshly ground black pepper

SPICY DIPPING SAUCE

½ cup mayonnaise

2 tablespoons sriracha

Zest and juice of ½ lime

1 clove garlic, minced

PER SERVING
580 CALORIES
39 G PROTEIN (27%)
8 G CARBS (5%)
44 G FAT (68%)   16 G SAT FAT
4 G FIBER

CLASSIC FISH STICKS
WITH TARTAR SAUCE

MAKES 4 SERVINGS

Fish sticks are a family favorite—and easy to make keto-friendly! Make sure you use dill pickles, not sweet pickles, which are loaded with sugar. If cod isn't available, feel free to substitute halibut in this recipe. Serve with Kohlrabi "Fries" (page 104) and steamed broccoli for a fish-and-chips style feast.

1½ pounds cod fillets, cut into 1-inch strips

1 teaspoon salt

½ teaspoon freshly ground black pepper

2 eggs

¾ cup almond flour

¼ cup grated Parmesan cheese

TARTAR SAUCE

½ cup sour cream

½ cup mayonnaise

3 tablespoons chopped dill pickle

2 tablespoons capers, drained and chopped

½ teaspoon dried dill

1 tablespoon dill pickle liquid (optional)

1. Preheat the air fryer to 400°F.

2. Season the cod with the salt and black pepper; set aside.

3. In a shallow bowl, lightly beat the eggs. In a second shallow bowl, combine the almond flour and Parmesan cheese. Stir until thoroughly combined.

4. Working with a few pieces at a time, dip the fish into the egg mixture followed by the flour mixture. Press lightly to ensure an even coating.

5. Working in batches if necessary, arrange the fish in a single layer in the air fryer basket and spray lightly with olive oil. Pausing halfway through the cooking time to turn the fish, air fry for 12 to 15 minutes, until the fish flakes easily with a fork. Let sit in the basket for a few minutes before serving with the tartar sauce.

6. To make the tartar sauce: In a small bowl, combine the sour cream, mayonnaise, pickle, capers, and dill. If you prefer a thinner sauce, stir in the pickle liquid.

PER SERVING
600 CALORIES
42 G PROTEIN (28%)
14 G CARBS (9%)
42 G FAT (63%)   8.5 G SAT FAT
2 G FIBER

SCALLOPS
IN LEMON-BUTTER SAUCE

Makes 2 Servings

If you've ever had tough scallops, you know how important it is to get tender results. Your air fryer is the perfect tool for this. Make sure to buy "dry" sea scallops, which haven't been treated with chemicals to make them retain water. When cooked, dry scallops have a more pleasant "sweet" flavor and are less likely to become tough. Serve with broccoli or asparagus for an amazing keto dinner.

8 large dry sea scallops
(about ¾ pound)

Salt and freshly ground black pepper

2 tablespoons olive oil

2 tablespoons unsalted
butter, melted

2 tablespoons chopped flat-leaf
parsley

1 tablespoon fresh lemon juice

2 teaspoons capers, drained
and chopped

1 teaspoon grated lemon zest

1 clove garlic, minced

1. Preheat the air fryer to 400°F.

2. Use a paper towel to pat the scallops dry. Sprinkle lightly with salt and pepper. Brush with the olive oil. Arrange the scallops in a single layer in the air fryer basket. Pausing halfway through the cooking time to turn the scallops, air fry for about 6 minutes until firm and opaque.

3. Meanwhile, in a small bowl, combine the oil, butter, parsley, lemon juice, capers, lemon zest, and garlic. Drizzle over the scallops just before serving.

PER SERVING
170 CALORIES
11 G PROTEIN (25%)
3 G CARBS (7%)
13 G FAT (68%) | 4.7 G SAT FAT
0 G FIBER

STUFFED FLOUNDER
FLORENTINE

Makes 4 Servings

Why break out a skillet that requires close tending? Your air fryer is the perfect match for sautéed vegetables and delicate flounder. As a bonus, the pine nuts toast beautifully as the appliance preheats, so no time or energy is wasted.

1. Place the pine nuts in a 6-cup baking dish that fits in your air fryer. Set the air fryer to 400°F and air fry for 4 minutes until the nuts are lightly browned and fragrant. Remove the baking dish from the air fryer, tip the nuts onto a plate to cool, and continue preheating the air fryer. When the nuts are cool enough to handle, chop them into fine pieces.

2. In the 6-cup baking dish, combine the oil, tomatoes, spinach, and garlic. Use tongs to toss until thoroughly combined. Air fry for 5 minutes until the tomatoes are softened and the spinach is wilted.

3. Transfer the vegetables to a bowl and stir in the toasted pine nuts. Season to taste with salt and freshly ground black pepper.

4. Place 1 tablespoon of the butter in the bottom of the baking dish. Lower the heat on the air fryer to 350°F.

5. Place the flounder on a clean work surface. Sprinkle both sides with salt and black pepper. Divide the vegetable mixture among the flounder filets and carefully roll up, securing with toothpicks.

6. Working in batches if necessary, arrange the filets seam-side down in the baking dish along with 1 tablespoon of water. Top the filets with remaining 1 tablespoon butter and sprinkle with a dash of paprika. Cover loosely with foil and air fry for 10 to 15 minutes until the fish is opaque and flakes easily with a fork. Remove the toothpicks before serving with the lemon wedges.

¼ cup pine nuts

2 tablespoons olive oil

½ cup chopped tomatoes

1 (6-ounce) bag spinach, coarsely chopped

2 cloves garlic, chopped

Salt and freshly ground black pepper

2 tablespoons unsalted butter, divided

4 flounder filets (about 1½ pounds)

Dash of paprika

½ lemon, sliced into 4 wedges

PER SERVING
390 CALORIES
29 G PROTEIN (30%)
2 G CARBS (2%)
29 G FAT (68%)   4.5 G SAT FAT
1 G FIBER

SESAME-CRUSTED SALMON

Sesame seeds give you the crust you crave without all the carbs. Use a mix of brown and black seeds for an impressive presentation. Wondering about the honey included in this recipe? No keto worries: 1 teaspoon for 4 servings provides a negligible amount of sugar while helping the sesame seeds coat the salmon.

1. Preheat the air fryer to 360°F.

2. Place the sesame seeds on a plate or in a small shallow bowl. In a separate small bowl, combine the soy sauce, sesame oil, and honey.

3. Brush all sides of the salmon with the soy sauce mixture until thoroughly coated. Press the top of each filet into the sesame seeds to create a coating.

4. Arrange the fish in a single layer in the basket of the air fryer, seed-side up. Air fry for 10 minutes until the fish is firm and flakes easily with a fork. Top with the marjoram, if desired, before serving.

¼ cup mixed black and brown sesame seeds

1 tablespoon reduced-sodium soy sauce

1 teaspoon sesame oil

1 teaspoon honey

4 (6-ounce) salmon filets, skin removed

2 tablespoons chopped fresh marjoram, for garnish (optional)

PER SERVING
310 CALORIES
35 G PROTEIN (46%)
3 G CARBS (4%)
17 G FAT (50%)   2.6 G SAT FAT
1 G FIBER

CUCUMBER AND SALMON SALAD

Light and crunchy cucumbers are the perfect complement to rich and tender salmon. Beyond the amazing taste, salmon provides valuable fats that can play an important role in heart health, so you may want to put this salad on a regular menu rotation.

1 pound salmon filet

1½ tablespoons olive oil, divided

1 tablespoon sherry vinegar

1 tablespoon capers, rinsed and drained

1 seedless cucumber, thinly sliced

¼ Vidalia onion, thinly sliced

2 tablespoons chopped fresh parsley

Salt and freshly ground black pepper

1. Preheat the air fryer to 400°F.

2. Lightly coat the salmon with ½ tablespoon of the olive oil. Place skin-side down in the air fryer basket and air fry for 8 to 10 minutes until the fish is opaque and flakes easily with a fork. Transfer the salmon to a plate and let cool to room temperature. Remove the skin and carefully flake the fish into bite-size chunks.

3. In a small bowl, whisk the remaining 1 tablespoon olive oil and the vinegar until thoroughly combined. Add the flaked fish, capers, cucumber, onion, and parsley. Season to taste with salt and freshly ground black pepper. Toss gently to coat. Serve immediately or cover and refrigerate for up to 4 hours.

PER SERVING
440 CALORIES
39 G PROTEIN (36%)
7 G CARBS (7%)
28 G FAT (58%)   5.3 SAT FAT
1 G FIBER

TUNA STEAKS
WITH OLIVE TAPENADE

MAKES 4 SERVINGS

Count down 10 minutes to terrific tuna when you use your air fryer! While it is cooking up flaky and delicious, make the simple yet super flavorful marinade. When preparing this recipe, remember to go easy on the salt. The saltiness of the tapenade will more than compensate for a light touch when preparing the tuna.

1. Preheat the air fryer to 400°F.

2. Drizzle the tuna steaks with the olive oil and sprinkle with salt and black pepper. Arrange the tuna steaks in a single layer in the air fryer basket. Pausing to turn the steaks halfway through the cooking time, air fry for 10 minutes until the fish is firm.

3. To make the tapenade: In a food processor fitted with a metal blade, combine the olives, olive oil, parsley, garlic, vinegar, and capers. Pulse until the mixture is finely chopped, pausing to scrape down the sides of the bowl if necessary. Spoon the tapenade over the top of the tuna steaks and serve with lemon wedges.

4 (6-ounce) ahi tuna steaks

1 tablespoon olive oil

Salt and freshly ground black pepper

½ lemon, sliced into 4 wedges

OLIVE TAPENADE

½ cup pitted kalamata olives

1 tablespoon olive oil

1 tablespoon chopped fresh parsley

1 clove garlic

2 teaspoons red wine vinegar

1 teaspoon capers, drained

PER SERVING
275 CALORIES
35 G PROTEIN (51%)
2 G CARBS (3%)
14 G FAT (46%)   2.2 G SAT FAT
1 G FIBER

TUNA PATTIES
WITH SPICY SRIRACHA SAUCE

Tuna patties make a very affordable alternative to crab cakes when your budget is stretched a little thin. And they're just as delicious and easy to make keto-friendly! If you're not a fan of spicy foods, try serving these patties with the lemon aioli recipe that's paired with the crab cakes (page 74).

2 (6-ounce) cans tuna packed in oil, drained

3 tablespoons almond flour

2 tablespoons mayonnaise

1 teaspoon dried dill

½ teaspoon onion powder

Pinch of salt and pepper

SPICY SRIRACHA SAUCE

¼ cup mayonnaise

1 tablespoon sriracha sauce

1 teaspoon garlic powder

1. Preheat the air fryer to 380°F. Line the basket with parchment paper.

2. In a large bowl, combine the tuna, almond flour, mayonnaise, dill, and onion powder. Season to taste with salt and freshly ground black pepper. Use a fork to stir, mashing with the back of the fork as necessary, until thoroughly combined.

3. Use an ice cream scoop to form the tuna mixture patties. Place the patties in a single layer on the parchment paper in the air fryer basket. Press lightly with the bottom of the scoop to flatten into a circle about ½ inch thick. Pausing halfway through the cooking time to turn the patties, air fry for 10 minutes until lightly browned.

4. To make the sriracha sauce: In a small bowl, combine the mayonnaise, sriracha, and garlic powder. Serve the tuna patties topped with the sriracha sauce.

PER SERVING
390 CALORIES
29 G PROTEIN (30%)
2 G CARBS (2%)
29 G FAT (68%)   4.5 G SAT FAT
1 G FIBER

VEGETARIAN

EGGPLANT LASAGNA

Air-fried eggplant slices in this recipe replace the heavy pasta noodles in a traditional lasagna. But you keep all of the creamy, cheesy filling. Using a 6-cup casserole dish in your air fryer fits perfectly and gives you reasonable portions that also fit within your ketogenic eating goals. So easy, so delicious!

1 small eggplant (about ¾ pound), sliced into rounds

2 teaspoons salt

1 tablespoon olive oil

1 cup shredded mozzarella, divided

1 cup ricotta cheese

1 large egg

¼ cup grated Parmesan cheese

½ teaspoon dried oregano

1½ cups no-sugar-added marinara

1 tablespoon chopped fresh parsley

1. Preheat the air fryer to 350°F. Coat a 6-cup casserole dish that fits in your air fryer with olive oil; set aside.

2. Arrange the eggplant slices in a single layer on a baking sheet and sprinkle with the salt. Let sit for 10 minutes. Use a paper towel to remove the excess moisture and salt.

3. Working in batches if necessary, brush the eggplant with the olive oil and arrange in a single layer in the air fryer basket. Pausing halfway through the cooking time to turn the eggplant, air fry for 6 minutes until softened. Transfer the eggplant back to the baking sheet and let cool.

4. In a small bowl, combine ½ cup of the mozzarella with the ricotta, egg, Parmesan, and oregano. To assemble the lasagna, spread a spoonful of marinara in the bottom of the casserole dish, followed by a layer of eggplant, a layer of the cheese mixture, and a layer of marinara. Repeat the layers until all of the ingredients are used, ending with the remaining ½ cup of mozzarella. Scatter the parsley on top. Cover the baking dish with foil.

5. Increase the air fryer to 370°F and air fry for 30 minutes. Uncover the dish and continue baking for 10 minutes longer until the cheese begins to brown. Let the casserole sit for at least 10 minutes before serving.

PER SERVING
350 CALORIES
20 G PROTEIN (23%)
17 G CARBS (20%)
22 G FAT (57%) 11.4 G SAT FAT
5 G FIBER

ZUCCHINI-RICOTTA TART

This light, keto-friendly tart is perfect for those lazy summer days when your garden yields more zucchini than you know what to do with. An added bonus: your air fryer delivers great results without heating up your kitchen.

1. Preheat the air fryer to 330°F. Coat a round 6-cup pan with olive oil and set aside.

2. In a large bowl, whisk ¼ cup of the Parmesan with the almond flour, coconut flour, garlic powder, and ¼ teaspoon of the salt. Stir in the melted butter until the dough resembles coarse crumbs. Press the dough firmly into the bottom and up the sides of the prepared pan. Air fry for 12 to 15 minutes until the crust begins to brown. Let cool to room temperature.

3. Meanwhile, place the zucchini in a colander and sprinkle with the remaining ½ teaspoon salt. Toss gently to distribute the salt and let sit for 30 minutes. Use paper towels to pat the zucchini dry.

4. In a large bowl, whisk together the ricotta, eggs, heavy cream, garlic, and tarragon. Gently stir in the zucchini slices. Pour the cheese mixture into the cooled crust and sprinkle with the remaining ¼ cup Parmesan.

5. Increase the air fryer to 350°F. Place the pan in the air fryer basket and air fry for 45 to 50 minutes, or until set and a tester inserted into the center of the tart comes out clean. Serve warm or at room temperature.

½ cup grated Parmesan cheese, divided

1½ cups almond flour

1 tablespoon coconut flour

½ teaspoon garlic powder

¾ teaspoon salt, divided

¼ cup unsalted butter, melted

1 zucchini, thinly sliced (about 2 cups)

1 cup ricotta cheese

3 eggs

2 tablespoons heavy cream

2 cloves garlic, minced

½ teaspoon dried tarragon

PER SERVING
390 CALORIES
19 G PROTEIN (19%)
14 G CARBS (14%)
30 G FAT (67%)   11.5 G SAT FAT
2 G FIBER

BUFFALO CAULIFLOWER BITES
WITH GARLIC BLUE CHEESE DIP

MAKES 4 SERVINGS

Wondering what to serve on game day that will keep you in a winning keto zone? These zippy cauliflower bites are just the ticket. Consider your air fryer the best game plan for flavor, ease, and all-around low-carb goodness in the kitchen.

1 large head cauliflower, chopped into florets

1 tablespoon olive oil

Salt and freshly ground black pepper

¼ cup unsalted butter, melted

¼ cup hot sauce

GARLIC BLUE CHEESE DIP

½ cup mayonnaise

¼ cup sour cream

2 tablespoons heavy cream

1 tablespoon fresh lemon juice

1 clove garlic, minced

¼ cup crumbled blue cheese

Salt and freshly ground black pepper

1. Preheat the air fryer to 400°F.

2. In a large bowl, combine the cauliflower and olive oil. Season to taste with salt and black pepper. Toss until the vegetables are thoroughly coated.

3. Working in batches, place half of the cauliflower in the air fryer basket. Pausing halfway through the cooking time to shake the basket, air fry for 8 to 10 minutes until the cauliflower is evenly browned. Transfer to a large bowl and repeat with the remaining cauliflower.

4. In a small bowl, whisk together the melted butter and hot sauce.

5. To make the dip: In a small bowl, combine the mayonnaise, sour cream, heavy cream, lemon juice, garlic, and blue cheese. Season to taste with salt and freshly ground black pepper.

6. Just before serving, pour the butter mixture over the cauliflower and toss gently until thoroughly coated. Serve with the dip on the side.

PER SERVING
510 CALORIES
7 G PROTEIN (5%)
13 G CARBS (10%)
50 G FAT (85%)   16.4 G SAT FAT
5 G FIBER

ALMOND-CAULIFLOWER GNOCCHI

MAKES 4 SERVINGS

Gnocchi are tender Italian-style dumplings that are traditionally made with all-purpose flour and potatoes. But this keto-friendly version, courtesy of your air fryer, lets you skip those unnecessary carbs with perfect results every time.

5 cups cauliflower florets

⅔ cup almond flour

½ teaspoon salt

¼ cup unsalted butter, melted

¼ cup grated Parmesan cheese

1. In a food processor fitted with a metal blade, pulse the cauliflower until finely chopped. Transfer the cauliflower to a large microwave-safe bowl and cover it with a paper towel. Microwave for 5 minutes. Spread the cauliflower on a towel to cool.

2. When cool enough to handle, draw up the sides of the towel and squeeze tightly over a sink to remove the excess moisture. Return the cauliflower to the food processor and whirl until creamy. Sprinkle in the flour and salt and pulse until a sticky dough comes together.

3. Transfer the dough to a workspace lightly floured with almond flour. Shape the dough into a ball and divide into 4 equal sections. Roll each section into a rope 1 inch thick. Slice the dough into squares with a sharp knife.

4. Preheat the air fryer to 400°F.

5. Working in batches if necessary, place the gnocchi in a single layer in the basket of the air fryer and spray generously with olive oil. Pausing halfway through the cooking time to turn the gnocchi, air fry for 25 to 30 minutes until golden brown and crispy on the edges. Transfer to a large bowl and toss with the melted butter and Parmesan cheese.

PER SERVING
360 CALORIES
9 G PROTEIN (13%)
14 G CARBS (21%)
20 G FAT (66%) | 8.3 G SAT FAT
4 G FIBER

CAULIFLOWER STEAK
WITH GREMOLATA

Makes 4 Servings

Cauliflower is so versatile! Here, thick "slices" sub for steak and are seasoned with a fresh sauce. Gremolata is an easy-to-make Italian herbal dressing that brightens up a variety of dishes—and it's very keto-friendly, so experiment by adding it to other dishes.

1. Preheat the air fryer to 400°F.

2. In a small bowl, combine the olive oil and Italian seasoning. Brush both sides of each cauliflower "steak" generously with the oil. Season to taste with salt and black pepper.

3. Working in batches if necessary, arrange the cauliflower in a single layer in the air fryer basket. Pausing halfway through the cooking time to turn the "steaks," air fry for 15 to 20 minutes until the cauliflower is tender and the edges begin to brown. Sprinkle with the Parmesan and air fry for 5 minutes longer.

4. To make the gremolata: In a food processor fitted with a metal blade, combine the parsley, garlic, and lemon zest and juice. With the motor running, add the olive oil in a steady stream until the mixture forms a bright green sauce. Season to taste with salt and black pepper. Serve the cauliflower steaks with the gremolata spooned over the top.

2 tablespoons olive oil

1 tablespoon Italian seasoning

1 large head cauliflower, outer leaves removed and sliced lengthwise through the core into thick "steaks"

Salt and freshly ground black pepper

¼ cup Parmesan cheese

GREMOLATA

1 bunch Italian parsley (about 1 cup packed)

2 cloves garlic

Zest of 1 small lemon, plus 1–2 teaspoons lemon juice

½ cup olive oil

Salt and pepper to taste

PER SERVING
390 CALORIES
7 G PROTEIN (7%)
14 G CARBS (14%)
36 G FAT (79%)   5.7 G SAT FAT
6 G FIBER

BROCCOLI-CHEESE FRITTERS

These light and crunchy fritters will satisfy with cheesy, garlicky flavor and 6 grams of fiber. When shopping for ranch dressing, remember that to keep this dish keto-friendly you'll need to avoid reduced-fat versions.

1. Preheat the air fryer to 400°F.

2. In a food processor fitted with a metal blade, pulse the broccoli until very finely chopped.

3. Transfer the broccoli to a large bowl and add the mozzarella, almond flour, ¼ cup of the flaxseed meal, baking powder, and garlic powder. Stir until thoroughly combined. Season to taste with salt and black pepper. Add the eggs and stir again to form a sticky dough. Shape the dough into 1¼-inch fritters.

4. Place the remaining ¼ cup flaxseed meal in a shallow bowl and roll the fritters in the meal to form an even coating.

5. Working in batches if necessary, arrange the fritters in a single layer in the basket of the air fryer and spray generously with olive oil. Pausing halfway through the cooking time to shake the basket, air fry for 20 to 25 minutes until the fritters are golden brown and crispy. Serve with the ranch dressing for dipping.

1 cup broccoli florets

1 cup shredded mozzarella cheese

¾ cup almond flour

½ cup flaxseed meal, divided

2 teaspoons baking powder

1 teaspoon garlic powder

Salt and freshly ground black pepper

2 eggs, lightly beaten

½ cup ranch dressing

PER SERVING
450 CALORIES
19 G PROTEIN (16%)
16 G CARBS (14%)
36 G FAT (70%)   7.8 G SAT FAT
6 G FIBER

CRISPY TOFU

Skip tending a hot wok! An air fryer is the perfect tool for making crispy blocks of tofu. Look for chili-garlic sauce in the Asian section of your grocery store. If you prefer less spicy food, use a few chopped cloves of garlic instead of the sauce. Enjoy crispy tofu on top of salads or alongside your favorite vegetables for a perfect plant-based protein.

1 (16-ounce) block extra-firm tofu

2 tablespoons reduced-sodium soy sauce

1 tablespoon toasted sesame oil

1 tablespoon olive oil

1 tablespoon chili-garlic sauce

1½ teaspoons black sesame seeds

1 scallion, thinly sliced

1. Press the tofu for at least 15 minutes by wrapping it in paper towels and setting a heavy pan on top so that the moisture drains.

2. Slice the tofu into bite-size cubes and transfer to a bowl. Drizzle with the soy sauce, sesame oil, olive oil, and chili-garlic sauce. Cover and refrigerate for 1 hour or up to overnight.

3. Preheat the air fryer to 400°F.

4. Arrange the tofu in a single layer in the air fryer basket. Pausing to shake the pan halfway through the cooking time, air fry for 15 to 20 minutes until crisp. Serve with any juices that accumulate in the bottom of the air fryer, sprinkled with the sesame seeds and sliced scallion.

PER SERVING
180 CALORIES
11 G PROTEIN (24%)
5 G CARBS (11%)
13 G FAT (65%)   1.7 G SAT FAT
1 G FIBER

MUSHROOM CAPS
STUFFED WITH SPINACH AND ARTICHOKES

This dish is the evolution of spinach-artichoke dip—all that creamy flavor packed into mushrooms that cook up tender in your air fryer! Be sure to use marinated artichoke hearts in this recipe—not those packed in water, because it's the oil that helps keep the nutrition values in the ketogenic range.

1. Preheat the air fryer to 400°F.

2. Rub the olive oil over the portobello mushrooms until thoroughly coated. Sprinkle both sides with the salt and black pepper. Place top-side down on a clean work surface.

3. In a small bowl, combine the goat cheese, artichoke hearts, and spinach. Mash with the back of a fork until thoroughly combined. Divide the cheese mixture among the mushrooms and sprinkle with the Parmesan cheese.

4. Air fry for 10 to 14 minutes until the mushrooms are tender and the cheese has begun to brown. Top with the fresh parsley just before serving.

2 tablespoons olive oil

4 large portobello mushrooms, stems removed and gills scraped out

½ teaspoon salt

¼ teaspoon freshly ground pepper

4 ounces goat cheese, crumbled

½ cup chopped marinated artichoke hearts

1 cup frozen spinach, thawed and squeezed dry

½ cup grated Parmesan cheese

2 tablespoons chopped fresh parsley

PER SERVING
270 CALORIES
8 G PROTEIN (11%)
11 G CARBS (16%)
23 G FAT (73%)   11.5 G SAT FAT
4 G FIBER

SIDES

KOHLRABI "FRIES"

A proud member of the cruciferous vegetable family that includes cabbage, broccoli, and cauliflower, kohlrabi is the lesser-known cousin. However, as a keto-friendly ingredient, it should be more widely known because it provides far fewer carbs than potatoes. When buying kohlrabi, choose small, firm bulbs about the size of a tennis ball.

2 pounds kohlrabi, peeled and cut into ¼–½-inch fries

2 tablespoons olive oil

Salt and freshly ground black pepper

1. Preheat the air fryer to 400°F.

2. In a large bowl, combine the kohlrabi and olive oil. Season to taste with salt and black pepper. Toss gently until thoroughly coated.

3. Working in batches if necessary, spread the kohlrabi in a single layer in the air fryer basket. Pausing halfway through the cooking time to shake the basket, air fry for 20 to 30 minutes until the fries are lightly browned and crunchy.

PER SERVING
120 CALORIES
4 G PROTEIN (12%)
14 G CARBS (41%)
7 G FAT (47%)   2.2 G SAT FAT
2 G FIBER

SPICY ROASTED BOK CHOY

Bok choy offers the perfect mix of a crisp head that holds its shape when cooked as well as tender greens at the end. In the air fryer, these qualities become more even pronounced. It's a side you can use to spice up a simple main.

2 tablespoons olive oil

2 tablespoons reduced-sodium soy sauce

2 teaspoons sesame oil

2 teaspoons chili-garlic sauce

2 cloves garlic, minced

1 head (about 1 pound) bok choy, sliced lengthwise into quarters

2 teaspoons black sesame seeds

1. Preheat the air fryer to 400°F.

2. In a large bowl, combine the olive oil, soy sauce, sesame oil, chili-garlic sauce, and garlic. Add the bok choy and toss, massaging the leaves with your hands if necessary, until thoroughly coated.

3. Arrange the bok choy in the basket of the air fryer. Pausing about halfway through the cooking time to shake the basket, air fry for 7 to 10 minutes until the bok choy is tender and the tips of the leaves begin to crisp. Remove from the basket and let cool for a few minutes before coarsely chopping. Serve sprinkled with the sesame seeds.

PER SERVING
100 CALORIES
2 G PROTEIN (8%)
4 G CARBS (17%)
8 G FAT (75%)   1.3 G SAT FAT
1 G FIBER

ROASTED BRUSSELS SPROUTS
WITH PECANS AND GORGONZOLA

MAKES 4 SERVINGS

Brussels sprouts never tasted better than coming out of your air fryer! Toasting nuts while your air fryer preheats is an easy way to speed your prep and maximize the flavor of your ingredients. If you're not a Gorgonzola fan, feta makes a good substitute.

1. Spread the pecans in a single layer of the air fryer and set the heat to 350°F. Air fry for 3 to 5 minutes until the pecans are lightly browned and fragrant. Transfer the pecans to a plate and continue preheating the air fryer, increasing the heat to 400°F.

2. In a large bowl, toss the Brussels sprouts with the olive oil and season with salt and black pepper to taste.

3. Working in batches if necessary, arrange the Brussels sprouts in a single layer in the air fryer basket. Pausing halfway through the baking time to shake the basket, air fry for 20 to 25 minutes until the sprouts are tender and starting to brown on the edges.

4. Transfer the sprouts to a serving bowl and top with the toasted pecans and Gorgonzola. Serve warm or at room temperature.

½ cup pecans

1½ pounds fresh Brussels sprouts, trimmed and quartered

2 tablespoons olive oil

Salt and freshly ground black pepper

¼ cup crumbled Gorgonzola cheese

PER SERVING
250 CALORIES
9 G PROTEIN (13%)
17 G CARBS (25%)
19 G FAT (62%)   3.4 G SAT FAT
8 G FIBER

BACON-WRAPPED ASPARAGUS

MAKES 4 SERVINGS

Even if you're not a vegetable lover, you'll appreciate roasted asparagus that gets a crispy boost when it's wrapped in bacon. And it simply couldn't be easier to make in your air fryer! If large stalks of asparagus aren't available, wrap each piece of bacon around two or three thinner stalks.

1. Preheat the air fryer to 350°F.

2. Wrap a half piece of bacon around the center of each stalk of asparagus.

3. Working in batches, if necessary, arrange seam-side down in a single layer in the air fryer basket. Cook for 10 minutes until the bacon is crisp and the stalks are tender.

8 slices reduced-sodium bacon, cut in half

16 thick (about 1 pound) asparagus spears, trimmed of woody ends

PER SERVING
110 CALORIES
8 G PROTEIN (28%)
5 G CARBS (17%)
7 G FAT (55%)   2 G SAT FAT
2 G FIBER

ROASTED GREEN BEAN CASSEROLE

You don't need to wait until Thanksgiving to enjoy this classic side dish. With an air fryer at your disposal, you can whip up a batch of this cheesy, low-carb casserole any time. If fresh green beans aren't available, frozen whole beans (no need to thaw) work just as well. Just add another minute or two to your cooking time.

1 pound fresh green beans, ends trimmed, strings removed, and chopped into 2-inch pieces

1 (8-ounce) package sliced brown mushrooms

½ onion, sliced

1 clove garlic, minced

1 tablespoon olive oil

½ teaspoon salt

¼ teaspoon freshly ground black pepper

4 ounces cream cheese

½ cup chicken stock

¼ teaspoon ground nutmeg

½ cup grated Cheddar cheese

1. Preheat the air fryer to 400°F. Coat a 6-cup casserole dish with olive oil and set aside.

2. In a large bowl, combine the green beans, mushrooms, onion, garlic, olive oil, salt, and pepper. Toss until the vegetables are thoroughly coated with the oil and seasonings.

3. Transfer the mixture to the air fryer basket. Pausing halfway through the cooking time to shake the basket, air fry for 10 minutes until tender.

4. While the vegetables are cooking, in a 2-cup glass measuring cup, warm the cream cheese and chicken stock in the microwave on high for 1 to 2 minutes until the cream cheese is melted. Add the nutmeg and whisk until smooth.

5. Transfer the vegetables to the prepared casserole dish and pour the cream cheese mixture over the top. Top with the Cheddar cheese. Air fry for another 10 minutes until the cheese is melted and beginning to brown.

PER SERVING
250 CALORIES
10 G PROTEIN (15%)
14 G CARBS (21%)
19 G FAT (64%) | 9 G SAT FAT
4 G FIBER

FRIED ZUCCHINI SALAD

This simple side salad sings with the refreshing flavors of the Mediterranean. It's a perfect low-carb accompaniment to chicken or salmon. You'll love the crisp zucchini slices your air fryer produces.

1. Preheat the air fryer to 400°F.

2. In a large bowl, toss the zucchini slices with 1 tablespoon of the olive oil.

3. Working in batches if necessary, arrange the zucchini slices in an even layer in the air fryer basket. Pausing halfway through the cooking time to shake the basket, air fry for 5 to 7 minutes until soft and lightly browned on each side.

4. Meanwhile, in a small bowl, combine the remaining 4 tablespoons olive oil, parsley, mint, lemon zest, lemon juice, and garlic.

5. Arrange the zucchini on a plate and drizzle with the dressing. Sprinkle the feta and black pepper on top. Serve warm or at room temperature.

2 medium zucchini, thinly sliced

5 tablespoons olive oil, divided

¼ cup chopped fresh parsley

2 tablespoons chopped fresh mint

Zest and juice of ½ lemon

1 clove garlic, minced

¼ cup crumbled feta cheese

Freshly ground black pepper

PER SERVING
195 CALORIES
3 G PROTEIN (6%)
5 G CARBS (10%)
19 G FAT (84%)   4 G SAT FAT
1 G FIBER

ZUCCHINI FRITTERS

MAKES 4 SERVINGS

Forget the carb-laden bread! These fritters give you a delicious, keto-friendly way to enjoy zucchini, air fried with pantry ingredients you'll likely to already have on hand. For the best browning, be sure to use a piece of parchment paper cut slightly smaller than the bottom of the basket.

2 zucchini, grated (about 1 pound)

1 teaspoon salt

¼ cup almond flour

¼ cup grated Parmesan cheese

1 large egg

¼ teaspoon dried thyme

¼ teaspoon ground turmeric

¼ teaspoon freshly ground black pepper

1 tablespoon olive oil

½ lemon, sliced into wedges

1. Preheat the air fryer to 400°F. Cut a piece of parchment paper to fit slightly smaller than the bottom of the air fryer.

2. Place the zucchini in a large colander and sprinkle with the salt. Let sit for 5 to 10 minutes. Squeeze as much liquid as you can from the zucchini and place in a large mixing bowl. Add the almond flour, Parmesan, egg, thyme, turmeric, and black pepper. Stir gently until thoroughly combined.

3. Shape the mixture into 8 patties and arrange on the parchment paper. Brush lightly with the olive oil. Pausing halfway through the cooking time to turn the patties, air fry for 10 minutes until golden brown. Serve warm with the lemon wedges.

PER SERVING
190 CALORIES
6 G PROTEIN (12%)
8 G CARBS (16%)
16 G FAT (72%) | 2.8 G SAT FAT
2 G FIBER

ROASTED CURRY CAULIFLOWER

Tender roasted cauliflower is the chameleon of the vegetable world, taking on the vibrant color and flavor of its seasonings, and it makes an excellent low-carb side or main dish. An added bonus of roasting your cauliflower in an air fryer instead of on a sheet pan the old-fashioned way? It's far easier to give the basket of an air fryer a quick shake halfway through the cooking time.

1. Preheat the air fryer to 400°F.

2. In a large bowl, combine the olive oil, curry powder, salt, and pepper. Add the cauliflower and onion. Toss gently until the vegetables are completely coated with the oil mixture. Transfer the vegetables to the basket of the air fryer.

3. Pausing about halfway through the cooking time to shake the basket, air fry for 20 minutes until the cauliflower is tender and beginning to brown. Top with the parsley, if desired, before serving.

¼ cup olive oil

2 teaspoons curry powder

½ teaspoon salt

¼ teaspoon freshly ground black pepper

1 head cauliflower, cut into bite-size florets

½ red onion, sliced

2 tablespoons freshly chopped parsley, for garnish (optional)

PER SERVING
165 CALORIES
3 G PROTEIN (7%)
10 G CARBS (22%)
14 G FAT (71%)   2 G SAT FAT
4 G FIBER

ROASTED BROCCOLI
WITH SESAME DRESSING

MAKES 4 SERVINGS

Add Asian flair any night of the week—without turning to takeout! Roasting the broccoli in your air fryer will render the stems tender, but the florets will become slightly crunchy—all the better for holding on to as much of the delicious dressing as possible.

6 cups broccoli florets, cut into bite-size pieces

1 tablespoon olive oil

¼ teaspoon salt

2 tablespoons sesame seeds

2 tablespoons rice vinegar

2 tablespoons reduced-sodium soy sauce

2 tablespoons sesame oil

½ teaspoon Swerve sugar replacement

¼ teaspoon red pepper flakes (optional)

1. Preheat the air fryer to 400°F.

2. In a large bowl, toss the broccoli with the olive oil and salt until thoroughly coated.

3. Transfer the broccoli to the air fryer basket. Pausing halfway through the cooking time to shake the basket, air fry for 10 minutes until the stems are tender and the edges are beginning to crisp.

4. Meanwhile, in the same large bowl, whisk together the sesame seeds, vinegar, soy sauce, sesame oil, Swerve, and red pepper flakes (if using).

5. Transfer the broccoli to the bowl and toss until thoroughly coated with the seasonings. Serve warm or at room temperature.

PER SERVING
180 CALORIES
5 G PROTEIN (10%)
14 G CARBS (29%)
13 G FAT (61%)   1.8 SAT FAT
4 G FIBER

FRIED GREEN TOMATO SALAD
WITH BUTTERMILK DRESSING

MAKES 4 SERVINGS

This salad captures so much summer flavor in a keto-friendly, air-fried package! If allergies are a concern, it's easy to swap out the peanut flour for another low-carb choice; crushed pork rinds work as a flavorful substitute.

1. Preheat the air fryer to 400°F.

2. Slice the tomatoes into ½-inch slices and sprinkle with the salt. Let sit for 5 to 10 minutes.

3. Place the egg in a small shallow bowl. In another small shallow bowl, combine the peanut flour and Creole seasoning. Dip each tomato slice into the egg wash, then dip into the peanut flour mixture, turning to coat evenly.

4. Working in batches if necessary, arrange the tomato slices in a single layer in the air fryer basket and spray both sides lightly with olive oil. Air fry until browned and crisp, 8 to 10 minutes.

5. To make the buttermilk dressing: In a small bowl, whisk together the mayonnaise, sour cream, lemon juice, parsley, dill, chives, salt, garlic powder, and onion powder.

6. Serve the tomato slices on top of a bed of the arugula with the dressing on the side.

4 green tomatoes

½ teaspoon salt

1 large egg, lightly beaten

½ cup peanut flour

1 tablespoon Creole seasoning

1 (5-ounce) bag arugula

BUTTERMILK DRESSING

1 cup mayonnaise

½ cup sour cream

2 teaspoons fresh lemon juice

2 tablespoons finely chopped fresh parsley

1 teaspoon dried dill

1 teaspoon dried chives

½ teaspoon salt

½ teaspoon garlic powder

½ teaspoon onion powder

PER SERVING
560 CALORIES
9 G PROTEIN (6%)
16 G CARBS (11%)
54 G FAT (83%) 10.2 G SAT FAT
3 G FIBER

AIR-FRIED OKRA

This guilt-free version of a classic Southern side dish cuts carbs but not flavor! It's perfect served alongside roasted pork or air-fried chicken. Be sure to use fresh okra, which is usually available year-round, though the peak season is in the fall.

1 egg

½ cup milk

½ cup crushed pork rinds

¼ cup grated Parmesan cheese

¼ cup almond flour

1 teaspoon garlic powder

¼ teaspoon freshly ground black pepper

½ pound fresh okra, stems removed and chopped into 1-inch slices

1. Preheat the air fryer to 400°F.

2. In a shallow bowl, whisk together the egg and milk.

3. In a second shallow bowl, combine the pork rinds, Parmesan, almond flour, garlic powder, and black pepper.

4. Working with a few slices at a time, dip the okra into the egg mixture followed by the crumb mixture. Press lightly to ensure an even coating.

5. Working in batches if necessary, arrange the okra in a single layer in the air fryer basket and spray lightly with olive oil. Pausing halfway through the cooking time to turn the okra, air fry for 10 minutes until tender and golden brown. Serve warm.

PER SERVING

180 CALORIES

14 G PROTEIN (31%)

9 G CARBS (20%)

10 G FAT (49%)   3.1 G SAT FAT

2 G FIBER

SNACKS

DRY RUB CHICKEN WINGS

Chicken wings can be a part of a ketogenic eating plan thanks to the naturally high fat content of chicken skin. Fortunately, they also taste great! And with this spice rub, there's no need to slather them with sugary barbecue sauces when they come out of the air fryer.

1 tablespoon paprika

1 tablespoon Swerve sugar replacement

½ teaspoon dried oregano

½ teaspoon garlic powder

½ teaspoon freshly ground black pepper

½ teaspoon cayenne

1 pound chicken wings, tips removed

1. In a large bowl, combine the paprika, Swerve, oregano, garlic powder, black pepper, and cayenne. Add the chicken wings and toss until thoroughly coated. Cover and refrigerate for at least 1 hour or up to 8 hours.

2. Preheat the air fryer to 400°F.

3. Working in batches if necessary, arrange the wings in a single layer in the air fryer basket. Spray lightly with olive oil. Pausing halfway through the cooking time to turn the wings, air fry for 35 to 40 minutes until browned and crispy and a thermometer inserted into the thickest part registers 165°F.

PER SERVING
290 CALORIES
27 G PROTEIN (38%)
1 G CARBS (2%)
19 G FAT (60%)   5.7 G SAT FAT
1 G FIBER

CHEESE CRISPS

When you're hungry for a crunchy, salty snack, these cheesy bites are the perfect keto solution. Plus, they're far more economical and lower in carbs when prepared at home in your air fryer compared to the store-bought versions.

½ cup shredded Cheddar cheese

1 egg white

1. Preheat the air fryer to 400°F. Place a piece of parchment paper in the bottom of the air fryer basket.

2. In a medium bowl, combine the cheese and egg white, stirring with a fork until thoroughly combined.

3. Place small scoops of the cheese mixture in a single layer in the basket of the air fryer (about 1 inch apart). Use the fork to spread the mixture as thin as possible. Air fry for 10 to 12 minutes until the crisps are golden brown. Let cool for a few minutes before transferring them to a plate. Store at room temperature in an airtight container for up to 3 days.

PER SERVING
120 CALORIES
9 G PROTEIN (28%)
1 G CARBS (3%)
10 G FAT (69%)   5.5 G SAT FAT
0 G FIBER

CAJUN-SPICED KALE CHIPS

You've never tasted kale like this! There are several varieties of kale available, and all of them will work in this recipe. However, opt for a flat-leaf kale, such as Lacinato, if you want chips that resemble traditional potato chips.

1. Preheat the air fryer to 360°F.

2. In a large bowl, combine the kale, olive oil, garlic powder, and Creole seasoning. Toss until the kale is thoroughly coated.

3. Working in batches, arrange about 2 cups of the kale in an even layer in the basket of the air fryer. (Allow the mixture to stay as fluffy as possible to help air circulate in the basket.) Pausing halfway through to shake the basket, air fry for 8 to 10 minutes. Spread the kale chips on a baking sheet to cool completely. Repeat with the remaining kale. Store in an airtight container at room temperature for up to 2 days.

1 large bunch kale, stems removed and torn into chip-size pieces (about 6 cups)

2 tablespoons olive oil

1 teaspoon garlic powder

1 teaspoon Creole seasoning

PER SERVING
150 CALORIES
2 G PROTEIN (5%)
5 G CARBS (13%)
14 G FAT (82%)   2 G SAT FAT
2 G FIBER

KETO MOZZARELLA STICKS

Coated in bread crumbs and deep fried, traditionally prepared mozzarella sticks are rarely recommended as part of a weight loss plan. But they're a surprisingly smart keto snack when you pair almond flour and your air fryer to create a crispy low-carb coating.

1. In a shallow bowl, combine the almond flour, Parmesan, Italian seasoning, and garlic powder.

2. In a separate shallow bowl, whisk the egg.

3. Working one at a time, dip the mozzarella sticks in the egg wash and then roll in the almond flour mixture, pressing lightly to coat evenly. Arrange the mozzarella sticks on a plate lined with parchment paper. Freeze for 30 minutes.

4. Preheat the air fryer to 400°F.

5. Arrange the mozzarella sticks in a single layer in the air fryer basket. Spray generously with olive oil. Air fry for 5 minutes until the coating is browned. Let stand for 1 minute before removing to a plate.

¼ cup almond flour

¼ cup grated Parmesan cheese

½ teaspoon Italian seasoning

¼ teaspoon garlic powder

1 egg

6 part-skim mozzarella sticks, cut in half

PER SERVING
210 CALORIES
16 G PROTEIN (30%)
5 G CARBS (10%)
14 G FAT (60%)   6.7 G SAT FAT
1 G FIBER

BACON AND EGG BITES

Bacon and eggs aren't just a perfect pairing for breakfast. These savory bites prove they can make quite a filling snack any time of day. They're one more way to enjoy the bacon that crisps up perfectly and easily in your air fryer.

6 ounces (about 9 slices) reduced-sodium bacon

2 hard-boiled eggs, chopped

Flesh of ½ avocado, chopped

2 tablespoons unsalted butter, softened

2 tablespoons mayonnaise

1 jalapeño pepper, seeded and finely chopped

2 tablespoons chopped fresh cilantro

Juice of ½ lime

Salt and freshly ground black pepper

1. Arrange the bacon in a single layer in the air fryer basket (it's OK if the bacon sits a bit on the sides). Set the air fryer to 350°F and cook for 10 minutes. Check for crispiness and cook for 2 to 3 minutes longer if needed. Transfer the bacon to a paper towel–lined plate and let cool completely. Reserve 2 tablespoons of bacon grease from the bottom of the air fryer basket. Finely chop the bacon and set aside in a small, shallow bowl.

2. In a large bowl, combine the eggs, avocado, butter, mayonnaise, jalapeño, cilantro, and lime juice. Mash into a smooth paste with a fork or potato smasher. Season to taste with salt and pepper.

3. Add the reserved bacon grease to the egg mixture and stir gently until thoroughly combined. Cover and refrigerate for 30 minutes, or until the mixture is firm.

4. Divide the mixture into 12 equal portions and shape into balls. Roll the balls in the chopped bacon bits until completely coated.

PER SERVING (3 BALLS)
330 CALORIES
10 G PROTEIN (12%)
2 G CARBS (3%)
31 G FAT (85%) | 10.6 G SAT FAT
0 G FIBER

BACON-PICKLE BITES

MAKES 4 SERVINGS

Salty, savory, and satisfying with only three ingredients, bacon-wrapped pickles may seem like an odd combination—only until you take your very first bite. Be sure to use dill pickles (not sweet pickles) to avoid added sugar.

1. Slice each pickle into 4 spears by cutting lengthwise. Wrap a piece of bacon around each pickle spear.

2. Arrange the pickles seam-side down in a single layer in the air fryer basket. Set the air fryer to 350°F and air fry for 10 minutes. Check for crispiness and cook for 2 to 3 minutes longer if needed. Serve with the ranch dressing for dipping.

4 dill pickles

8 slices reduced-sodium bacon, cut in half

¼ cup ranch dressing

PER SERVING
230 CALORIES
7 G PROTEIN (12%)
5 G CARBS (8%)
21 G FAT (80%)   4.4 G SAT FAT
1 G FIBER

BACON-WRAPPED
JALAPEÑO POPPERS

While drinking alcohol doesn't fit into a ketogenic diet, there's no reason you can't still enjoy a bar food snack like these jalapeño poppers. Using the right ingredients helps you stay on a low-carb track while enjoying a healthier happy hour.

4 ounces cream cheese, softened

1 tablespoon hot sauce

1 teaspoon garlic powder

8 jalapeño peppers, halved lengthwise and seeded

8 slices reduced-sodium bacon, cut in half

1. In a small bowl, combine the cream cheese, hot sauce, and garlic powder.

2. Fill the pepper halves with equal amounts of the cream cheese mixture and wrap each pepper tightly with a half piece of bacon to enclose the ingredients. For best results, make sure the ends of the bacon are on the bottom of the peppers.

3. Arrange the peppers cut-side up in a single layer in the air fryer basket. Set the air fryer to 350°F and air fry for 15 to 20 minutes until the peppers are softened and the bacon is crisp. Let cool slightly before serving.

PER SERVING
190 CALORIES
8 G PROTEIN (16%)
4 G CARBS (8%)
17 G FAT (76%)   7.7 G SAT FAT
1 G FIBER

CHEESY SAUSAGE BITES

MAKES 12 SERVINGS

These bite-size balls of cheesy goodness are the perfect take-along for a party. If an air fryer isn't available at your destination, cook them ahead of time and warm them up for a few minutes in a regular oven. It's likely they'll all disappear before the serving plate cools.

1 pound bulk Italian sausage

½ cup almond flour

¼ cup coconut flour

1 teaspoon garlic powder

½ teaspoon baking powder

½ teaspoon smoked paprika

½ teaspoon dried oregano

3 eggs

¼ cup coconut oil, melted

½ cup sour cream

2 cups shredded Cheddar cheese

1. Crumble the sausage into small pieces in the air fryer basket. Set the air fryer to 400°F and air fry for 10 to 15 minutes until browned. Transfer the sausage to a bowl and set aside. When the air fryer basket is cool enough to handle, drain the grease and wash the basket.

2. Meanwhile, in a small bowl, combine the almond flour, coconut flour, garlic powder, baking powder, paprika, and oregano.

3. In a large bowl, whisk together the eggs, coconut oil, and sour cream.

4. Add the flour mixture to the egg mixture. Use a silicone spatula to gently fold the ingredients until thoroughly combined (do not overmix). Stir in the reserved sausage and the Cheddar. Let the batter rest for 5 minutes.

5. Using a small cookie scoop, shape the dough into 24 balls and arrange them on a rimmed baking sheet. Refrigerate for 10 minutes.

6. Preheat the air fryer to 370°F.

7. Working in batches, arrange the balls in a single layer in the air fryer basket (about 1 inch apart). Spray generously with olive oil. Pausing halfway through the cooking time to shake the basket, air fry for 10 to 12 minutes until golden brown.

PER SERVING
280 CALORIES
13 G PROTEIN (19%)
4 G CARBS (6%)
23 G FAT (75%)   11.9 G SAT FAT
0 G FIBER

AVOCADO FRIES

Avocado fries are a special treat because they offer both crunchy and creamy goodness with every bite. You'll also get 7 grams of fiber per serving. Use avocados that are ripe but still firm; they will naturally soften a bit in the air fryer.

1. Preheat the air fryer to 400°F.

2. In a shallow bowl, combine the almond flour, Parmesan cheese, paprika, and garlic powder.

3. In a separate shallow bowl, whisk the eggs.

4. Working one at a time, dip the avocado wedges first in the egg and then dredge in the almond flour mixture, pressing lightly to coat evenly. Arrange the avocado fries on a plate lined with parchment paper.

5. Working in batches if necessary, arrange the avocado fries in a single layer in the air fryer basket, making sure they do not touch. Spray generously with olive oil. Pausing halfway through the cooking time to turn the fries, air fry for 7 to 8 minutes until the coating is brown and crispy. Serve with the lime wedges (if desired).

¼ cup almond flour

¼ cup grated Parmesan cheese

½ teaspoon smoked paprika

¼ teaspoon garlic powder

2 eggs

Flesh of 3 avocados, each sliced into 8 pieces (24 wedges total)

Salt and freshly ground black pepper

4 lime wedges, for garnish (optional)

PER SERVING
270 CALORIES
9 G PROTEIN (13%)
12 G CARBS (17 %)
22 G FAT (70%)   3.9 G SAT FAT
7 G FIBER

ZUCCHINI FRIES
WITH MARINARA

MAKES 4 SERVINGS

You'll never miss French fries once you get the hang of these low-carb zucchini sticks. A quick spritz of olive oil is all your air fryer requires to make a perfectly crispy coating. Many prepared marinara sauces contain added sugar, so read the ingredient labels carefully when selecting one.

1. Preheat the air fryer to 400°F.

2. Slice the zucchini in half, lengthwise, and then into sticks about ½ inch thick and 4 inches long.

3. In a shallow bowl, combine the almond flour, Parmesan, Italian seasoning, garlic powder (if using), salt, and pepper.

4. In another shallow bowl, whisk the egg with a fork until lightly beaten.

5. Dip the zucchini into the egg mixture and then dredge in the almond flour mixture. Arrange in the air fryer basket, making sure the pieces do not touch (work in batches if necessary). Generously spray the zucchini with olive oil.

6. Air fry for 10 minutes, turning halfway through the cooking time and spraying with more oil, until crispy. Meanwhile, warm the marinara in the microwave. Serve the zucchini sticks with the marinara sauce.

2 zucchini

½ cup almond flour

½ cup grated Parmesan cheese

1 teaspoon Italian seasoning

½ teaspoon garlic powder (optional)

Pinch of salt and pepper

1 large egg

1 cup no-sugar-added marinara sauce

PER SERVING
210 CALORIES
12 G PROTEIN (23%)
16 G CARBS (30%)
11 G FAT (47%)   2.4 G SAT FAT
4 G FIBER

DESSERTS

GUILT-FREE
CHOCOLATE CHIP COOKIES

With only 14 grams of carbs per cookie, these treats can fit into a keto-friendly eating plan. Another bonus: they're ready quickly! Cooking them in your air fryer means a small batch finishes faster than in a conventional oven. Be sure to let the cookies cool in the basket before transferring them; they are extremely fragile when hot.

2 cups almond flour

¼ cup Swerve sugar replacement

Scant ½ teaspoon salt

¼ teaspoon baking soda

½ cup sugar-free chocolate chips

½ cup chopped pecans

¼ cup coconut oil

1 teaspoon vanilla extract

2 tablespoons milk, as needed

1. Line the air fryer basket with parchment paper and preheat the air fryer to 300°F.

2. In a large bowl, combine the almond flour, Swerve, salt, baking soda, chocolate chips, and pecans. Add the coconut oil and vanilla extract and stir until thoroughly combined. Add the milk, a teaspoon or two at a time as needed, until the mixture forms a stiff dough.

3. Roll the dough into 12 equal-size balls. Flatten slightly to form cookie-shaped disks. Arrange the cookies in the basket, in batches if necessary, so they don't touch.

4. Air fry for 8 to 10 minutes until the cookies begin to brown. Cool completely before removing from the air fryer (the cookies will harden as they cool).

PER SERVING (1 COOKIE)
225 CALORIES
6 G PROTEIN (10%)
14 G CARBS (23%)
18 G FAT (67%)   6 G SAT FAT
2 G FIBER

CREAM CHEESE COOKIES

The beauty of the air fryer is that it allows you to cook small batches easily. This recipe makes enough dough for 48 cookies, but you don't have to cook them all at once. Shape the cookies, arrange on a parchment paper–lined baking sheet, and freeze. Once solid, transfer them to a resealable freezer bag where they'll keep for up to 1 month; simply air fry a few minutes longer whenever you want to enjoy a treat straight from the freezer.

½ cup unsalted butter, softened

4 ounces plain cream cheese, softened

1 cup Swerve sugar replacement

2 eggs

1 tablespoon vanilla extract

1 teaspoon salt

6 cups almond flour

1. Line the air fryer basket with parchment paper and preheat the air fryer to 350°F.

2. In a stand mixer fitted with a paddle attachment, beat the butter, cream cheese, and Swerve until fluffy. Beat in the eggs, vanilla extract, and salt. Set the mixer to the lowest speed and slowly add the almond flour, ½ cup at a time, until thoroughly combined. (The dough will be dense and crumbly.)

3. Working in batches, roll a spoonful of dough into a ball, flatten it between your palms, and arrange in the air fryer (leave enough space between the cookies so they don't touch). Air fry for 12 to 15 minutes until the edges are lightly golden. Cool completely before removing from the air fryer (the cookies will harden as they cool).

PER SERVING (1 COOKIE)
110 CALORIES
4 G PROTEIN (15%)
5 G CARBS (19%)
8 G FAT (66%)   1.7 G SAT FAT
1 G FIBER

PEANUT BUTTER COOKIES

MAKES 12 COOKIES

If you're a peanut butter fan, this keto version of a classic cookie is sure to become your go-to recipe. Three ingredients that are easy to keep on hand and just minutes in your air fryer means you'll have cookies anytime a craving strikes! What could be easier?

1. Line the air fryer basket with parchment paper and preheat the air fryer to 350°F.

2. In a stand mixer fitted with a paddle attachment, beat the peanut butter and Swerve until fluffy. Beat in the egg.

3. Working in batches, roll a spoonful of dough into a ball, arrange in the air fryer basket, and use the back of a fork to flatten the cookies and make the traditional crisscross pattern. (Leave enough space between the cookies so they don't touch when flattened.) Air fry for 12 to 15 minutes until the edges are lightly golden. Cool completely before removing from the air fryer (the cookies will harden as they cool).

½ cup peanut butter

½ cup Swerve sugar replacement

1 egg

PER SERVING (1 COOKIE)
140 CALORIES
6 G PROTEIN (16%)
5 G CARBS (13%)
12 G FAT (71%)   2 G SAT FAT
1 G FIBER

DOUBLE CHOCOLATE
BROWNIES

Makes 8 Servings

Baking brownies in a cake pan may seem unconventional, but round pans tend to fit better in air fryers. Of course, if your air fryer can accommodate a traditional square pan, by all means use it. Whatever shape your brownies are, the results will be moist and delicious!

1. Preheat the air fryer to 350°F. Line an 8-inch cake pan with parchment paper and brush with vegetable oil.

2. In a large bowl, combine the almond flour, cocoa powder, baking powder, Swerve, and salt. Add the butter, eggs, and vanilla. Stir until thoroughly combined. (The batter will be thick.) Spread the batter into the prepared pan and scatter the chocolate chips on top.

3. Air fry for 15 to 20 minutes until the edges are set. (The center should still appear slightly undercooked.) Let cool completely before slicing. To store, cover and refrigerate the brownies for up to 3 days.

1 cup almond flour

½ cup unsweetened cocoa powder

½ teaspoon baking powder

⅓ cup Swerve sugar replacement

¼ teaspoon salt

½ cup unsalted butter, melted and cooled

3 eggs

1 teaspoon vanilla extract

2 tablespoons mini semisweet chocolate chips

PER SERVING
230 CALORIES
8 G PROTEIN (13%)
10 G CARBS (16%)
20 G FAT (71%)   9 G SAT FAT
3 G FIBER

CINNAMON CUPCAKES
WITH CREAM CHEESE FROSTING

Makes 6 Servings

This recipe is perfect for a special occasion. Six gorgeous cupcakes, enough to share with friends, will satisfy your sweet tooth without overstaying their welcome. Go ahead, and enjoy a keto-compatible cupcake!

½ cup plus 2 tablespoons almond flour

2 tablespoons low-carb vanilla protein powder

⅛ teaspoon salt

1 teaspoon baking powder

¼ teaspoon ground cinnamon

¼ cup unsalted butter

¼ cup Swerve sugar replacement

2 eggs

½ teaspoon vanilla extract

2 tablespoons heavy cream

CREAM CHEESE FROSTING

4 ounces cream cheese, softened

2 tablespoons unsalted butter, softened

½ teaspoon vanilla extract

2 tablespoons powdered Swerve sugar replacement

1–2 tablespoons heavy cream

1. Preheat the air fryer to 320°F. Lightly coat 6 silicone muffin cups with vegetable oil and set aside.

2. In a medium bowl, combine the almond flour, protein powder, salt, baking powder, and cinnamon; set aside.

3. In a stand mixer fitted with a paddle attachment, beat the butter and Swerve until creamy. Add the eggs, vanilla, and heavy cream, and beat again until thoroughly combined. Add half the flour mixture at a time to the butter mixture, mixing after each addition, until you have a smooth, creamy batter.

4. Divide the batter evenly among the muffin cups, filling each one about three-fourths full. Arrange the muffin cups in the air fryer and air fry for 20 to 25 minutes, or until a toothpick inserted into the center of a cupcake comes out clean. Transfer the cupcakes to a rack and let cool completely.

5. To make the cream cheese frosting: In a stand mixer fitted with a paddle attachment, beat the cream cheese, butter, and vanilla until fluffy. Add the Swerve and mix again until thoroughly combined. With the mixer running, add the heavy cream a tablespoon at a time until the frosting is smooth and creamy. Frost the cupcakes as desired.

PER SERVING
280 CALORIES
8 G PROTEIN (11%)
6 G CARBS (9%)
25 G FAT (80%)   12.7 G SAT FAT
1 G FIBER

SALTED CHOCOLATE CAKE

A rich, chocolate dessert for two in under 15 minutes? That's the beauty of cooking in an air fryer! Although it tastes indulgent, this cake is keto-friendly and also serves up 3 grams of fiber for extra satisfaction.

1. Preheat the air fryer to 350°F. Coat a 2-cup baking dish or ramekin with vegetable oil and set aside.

2. In a small bowl, combine the egg, cocoa powder, water, Swerve, flaxseed meal, vegetable oil, baking powder, and vanilla. Stir until thoroughly combined. Transfer the mixture to the prepared baking dish and place in the air fryer basket. Sprinkle the top with a pinch of salt. Air fry for 8 to 9 minutes until the edges begin to firm.

3. Let the cake cool for a few minutes before taking it out of the air fryer basket. Serve warm, with whipped topping (if desired).

1 egg

2 tablespoons unsweetened cocoa powder

2 tablespoons water

2 tablespoons Swerve sugar replacement

1 tablespoon flaxseed meal

1 tablespoon vegetable oil

½ teaspoon baking powder

⅛ teaspoon vanilla extract

Pinch of salt

Sugar-free whipped topping (optional)

PER SERVING
130 CALORIES
5 G PROTEIN (14%)
5 G CARBS (14%)
12 G FAT (72%)   2 G SAT FAT
3 G FIBER

FRIED CHEESECAKE BITES

MAKES 16 BITES

What's better than cheesecake? Fried cheesecake! Store these perfectly portioned dessert bites in your freezer for up to a month and you'll always be just a few short minutes away from a bite of blissfulness.

8 ounces cream cheese, softened

½ cup plus 2 tablespoons Swerve sugar replacement, divided

4 tablespoons heavy cream, divided

½ teaspoon vanilla extract

½ cup almond flour

1. In a stand mixer fitted with a paddle attachment, beat the cream cheese, ½ cup of the Swerve, 2 tablespoons of the heavy cream, and the vanilla until smooth. Using a small ice-cream scoop, divide the mixture into 16 balls and arrange them on a rimmed baking sheet lined with parchment paper. Freeze for 45 minutes until firm.

2. Line the air fryer basket with parchment paper and preheat the air fryer to 350°F.

3. In a small shallow bowl, combine the almond flour with the remaining 2 tablespoons Swerve.

4. In another small shallow bowl, place the remaining 2 tablespoons cream.

5. One at a time, dip the frozen cheesecake balls into the cream and then roll in the almond flour mixture, pressing lightly to form an even coating. Arrange the balls in a single layer in the air fryer basket, leaving room between them. Air fry for 2 minutes until the coating is lightly browned.

PER SERVING (4 BALLS)
330 CALORIES
8 G PROTEIN (10%)
8 G CARBS (10%)
30 G FAT (80%) | 14.4 G SAT FAT
1 G FIBER

CHOCOLATE PEANUT BUTTER TART

Two favorite flavors come together in a low-carb crust to create this heavenly dessert that's amazingly in the keto zone. When shopping for ingredients, check the labels carefully to make sure there's no added sugar in the peanut butter or peanut flour.

1 cup almond flour

¼ cup Swerve sugar replacement

6 tablespoons coconut oil, melted, divided

1 teaspoon vanilla extract, divided

⅓ cup peanut flour

⅓ cup plus 1 tablespoon powdered Swerve sugar replacement, divided

¾ cup smooth peanut butter

6 ounces sugar-free chocolate chips

1. Preheat the air fryer to 350°F. Line an 8-inch round baking pan with parchment paper and set aside.

2. In a bowl, combine the almond flour and Swerve. Add 3 tablespoons of the melted coconut oil and ½ teaspoon of the vanilla. Stir, pressing with the back of a spoon or spatula, until a crumbly dough forms. Press the dough into the bottom of the prepared pan. Air fry for 10 minutes until the edges are golden. Cool for a few minutes until the top is firm and the pan is cool enough to handle.

3. Meanwhile, in a medium bowl, stir together the peanut flour and ⅓ cup of the powdered Swerve. Add the peanut butter and the remaining ½ teaspoon vanilla. Mix well, pressing with the back of a spoon or spatula, until thoroughly combined. Spread the peanut butter mixture into the pan, using the back of a silicone spatula to ensure an even layer.

4. In a medium microwavable bowl, combine the chocolate chips and the remaining 3 tablespoons coconut oil. Heat on high in the microwave for 1 to 2 minutes, stirring every 20 seconds, until completely melted. Whisk in the remaining 1 tablespoon powdered Swerve. Pour the chocolate over the peanut butter layer and spread evenly.

5. Let the tart cool completely, until the chocolate is solid, before cutting into wedges.

PER SERVING
340 CALORIES
9 G PROTEIN (10%)
19 G CARBS (22%)
27 G FAT (68%) | 12.4 G SAT FAT
3 G FIBER

LUSCIOUS COCONUT PIE

Even pies complete with crispy crusts work with the keto diet. The coconut crust in this ingenious recipe cooks deliciously in your air fryer. Another thing you'll love about this luscious pie: you only need one mixing bowl to whip it up.

1. Spread ¼ cup of the coconut in the bottom of an 8-inch pie plate and place in the air fryer basket. Set the air fryer to 350°F and air fry the coconut while the air fryer preheats, about 5 minutes, until golden brown. Transfer the coconut to a small bowl and set aside for garnish. Brush the pie plate with vegetable oil and set aside.

2. In a large bowl, combine the remaining 1 cup shredded coconut, eggs, milk, granulated Swerve, coconut flour, butter, vanilla, and salt. Whisk until smooth. Pour the batter into the prepared pie plate and air fry for 40 to 45 minutes, or until a toothpick inserted into the center of the pie comes out clean. (Check halfway through the baking time and rotate the pan, if necessary, for even baking.)

3. Remove the pie from the air fryer and place on a baking rack to cool completely. Garnish with the reserved toasted coconut and the powdered Swerve or sugar-free whipped topping, if desired. Cover and refrigerate leftover pie for up to 3 days.

1 cup plus ¼ cup unsweetened shredded coconut, divided

2 eggs

1½ cups milk

½ cup granulated Swerve sugar replacement

½ cup coconut flour

¼ cup unsalted butter, melted

1½ teaspoons vanilla extract

¼ teaspoon salt

2 tablespoons powdered Swerve sugar replacement (optional)

½ cup sugar-free whipped topping (optional)

PER SERVING
220 CALORIES
5 G PROTEIN (9%)
7 G CARBS (12%)
20 G FAT (79%)   13.9 G SAT FAT
3 G FIBER

AIR-FRIED DOUGHNUT BITES

It's true: doughnuts can fit into your keto diet with this low-carb makeover! The right ingredient replacements and your air fryer do all the work to lighten the results. Laced with orange zest and rolled in a cinnamon coating, these doughnut bites make a sweet treat you won't regret later.

1. Line a small baking sheet with parchment paper and set aside.

2. In a medium pot over medium-high heat, combine the water, 5 tablespoons of the butter, 2 tablespoons of the Swerve, and the salt. Bring the mixture to boil, whisking until the butter is melted. Remove from the heat and let cool for a few minutes.

3. In a large mixing bowl, whisk together the almond flour, coconut flour, baking powder, and orange zest. Add the dry ingredients to the water mixture in the pot. Stir briskly. The mixture should be the consistency of loose mashed potatoes.

4. In a small bowl, whisk the eggs and vanilla. Add the egg mixture to the pot and whisk until smooth. Let sit for 10 to 15 minutes until the dough thickens.

5. Transfer the dough to a resealable bag. Cut a ¼-inch tip from one corner of the bag. Squeeze about 20 1½-inch mounds onto parchment paper. Freeze for 45 minutes or until hard.

6. Preheat the air fryer to 400°F. Working in batches if necessary, air fry the doughnuts for 6 minutes until brown and crisp.

7. In a small shallow bowl, combine the cinnamon and the remaining 2 tablespoons Swerve. In another small, shallow microwavable bowl, melt the remaining 3 tablespoons butter in the microwave on high for 30 seconds to 1 minute. While the doughnuts are warm, brush with the melted butter and roll in the cinnamon-Swerve mixture. Serve warm.

¾ cup water

8 tablespoons unsalted butter, divided

4 tablespoons Swerve sugar replacement, divided

½ teaspoon salt

¾ cup almond flour

⅓ cup coconut flour

1 teaspoon baking powder

Zest of 1 orange

2 eggs

1 teaspoon vanilla extract

2 teaspoons ground cinnamon

PER SERVING (5 BITES)
240 CALORIES
6 G PROTEIN (10%)
6 G CARBS (10%)
22 G FAT (80%)   10.4 G SAT FAT
1 G FIBER

INDEX